The Modern Fire Officer

Communicate, Motivate, & Lead
Jared Vermeulen

Contents

Foreword

The firehouse is an amazing place. I think there is an argument to be made that every fire station around the world houses some of the craziest, funniest, caring, maddening, smart, athletic, opinionated, fraternal, and most impassioned people all in one place! Where else do you find a family that enjoys running into burning buildings for fun? We have a collective screw loose that is just as strong as our will to help the people around us.

Within the firehouse walls, I have never laughed so hard, eaten so well, or even grieved so much. As a fire crew, we spend up to a third of our lives together, responding to emergencies and performing the necessary day-to-day duties. For a long and illustrious career, the environment within the station must be healthy. As officers this falls squarely on our shoulders. It is an extremely important responsibility we undertake with people we may not have personally chosen but have been blessed to work with and call family.

This then leads to the question, how do you lead such a peculiar group of individuals who experience some of the most beautiful and horrific events imaginable within a 24-hour period, and then go home to their families? They not only experience that once, but for decades? The truth is no one has all the answers. However, I hope the insights and concepts that I have found through experiences, mentors, and my own blood, sweat, and tears can give you a short cut to finding and/or honing your skills as a fire department leader.

What you do matters and not just for your crew. You have an effect on your community and can make a difference in the quality of their lives. This, in turn, makes a difference in the quality of your life and the lives of your crew mates. The impact that your crew has on the community starts with the health of the team and how you lead them.

When responding to emergencies, the basic firefighter who leaves the station smiling will outwork and outshine any expert firefighter who leaves that same station frowning. Help the crew smile and the service that is provided internally and externally will be second to none, especially when they are well trained.

This book is not a step-by-step guide on how to master every minute detail of the officer role. Instead, it is meant to introduce you to ideas that may be new or perceived as "outside of the box" historically for a fire officer. I wanted this book to be pointed and easy to read. I did not want to fill its pages with war stories; I'm sure you have plenty of your own. Use this book to reflect on yourself, your own experiences, and different modes of leadership you can use within the fire department.

As a fire department leader, it is my goal that when my fellow firefighters see my name on the roster, they are excited to come into work, they know they will provide a great service, and get home safely. Take the ideas and concepts offered within these pages and make that a goal for you as well, if it is not already. We all have room for growth. Become a truly modern fire officer, a great leader, and a mentor.

Chapter One

A New View of Leadership

How do you define leadership? Let's get straight to the point, leadership is persuading a group of individuals to accomplish a task they may not necessarily want to do. It is as simple as that, right? I wish. At its core it is a simple definition, but in practice there are so many moving parts that it can become dizzying. Leadership is nuanced and encompasses many skills that are hard to understand, build, and master. Skills such as communication, psychology, self-awareness, etc. Each of these on their own could fill volumes!

You could liken becoming a leader to climbing a mountain. Standing at its basin, you may feel daunted staring up at the summit. There it is, miles away, sharp, raw, icy. Stop staring at it. Instead, envision the "line." The "line" is the route a climber prepares ahead of time by familiarizing themself with the dangers of the mountain face. With that information, the climber chooses the safest avenue of travel that matches their expertise level. You must prepare yourself and your team in the same manner.

There have been other "climbers" before you. Some of their paths can be recognized easily because the paths are well-traveled through the easy passages of the mountain's natural features. Some paths may require engineering and quick thinking when you arrive at a dangerous junction. This book will better prepare you to see the "line" and make the climb of firehouse leadership. It will help make the paths clearer to you, and hopefully guide you away from the pitfalls.

Remember, even when you reach the top, you have only mastered it for the day. The danger does not lessen with each climb, and the conditions you face are always subject to change. However, with each climb, you can always learn something new and find more efficient and advantageous ways to ascend.

Your perspectives will change constantly on the climb up, and your view from the top will look a lot different from the one you had below. Leadership is the same. Your perspectives will and must change to meet your current circumstances as you grow. Allow those changes to help shape you into a better officer. Never stop learning, never stop trying new methods to stay current and safe. The "mountain" of leadership can never be truly mastered, but you can make the summit and take pride in your hard work.

What Leadership Has Meant Historically Within the Firehouse

You may have preconceived notions about what leadership is according to what you may have experienced in your fire career so far. You may even have some ideas which you obtained in childhood, from a parent that raised you well or from another mentor who helped you to attain certain goals. These are excellent examples to meditate upon, not just for the things they did well but also in the areas they fell short. Taking as many examples as possible into consideration that you can personally pull from, along with understanding your own strengths and weaknesses, is key.

Historically, the archetype of leadership in the fire service has resembled a drill instructor from the armed forces: In your face, loud and in charge. A leader who has little care for the mental health of the subordinate and who skews more heavily toward the outcome of the incident. This may work in short bursts of actual battle or boot camp, but for maintaining a high-level of performance year after year, this leadership style will wane because the will of the employee will wane.

Yes, the fire service is paramilitary. Yes, we have a hierarchy. Yes, we need our subordinates to act in a timely matter to accomplish our goals safely. No, we are not the military. There are many similarities we share with armed forces, but at the end of the day we are non-deployed, volunteer or governmental employees, with many facets to our busy civilian lives.

There are times when we must raise our voice, be aggressive, and display our "command presence." However, this cannot be the constant state of mind of a great fire house leader. After a while, treating the majority of subordinates with constant aggression will prove itself detrimental in many aspects of their work.[1]

There is no healthy way to maintain that style of management for any lengthy period of time for you or your crew. How many cadets would graduate from boot camp if they were dealing with drill instructors for more than a few months? Can we expect our firefighters to deal with such tactics for a 30-year career?

I am here to tell you that leadership it something different than boot camp drill instructing. Great leaders observe and understand many intricate working parts simultaneously and orchestrate their interactions toward a common goal. The "working parts" is the knowledge we must possess, not just of our job and equipment, but of our crew. The common goal is high-quality customer and community service, reaching the vision of the department, and caring for the internal customer. This balancing act takes place all the time. A leader is a leader always. On and off emergency scenes, at the station, at training, and so on.

The Modern Officer

Service, Sacrifice, Self-Control, and Humility. Does the word leader come to mind when you read those words? By the time you finish reading this book, it is my hope that not only will you equate them to being a leader, but that you will understand those qualities to be the foundation of great leadership. No doubt this may be in direct opposition to everything you've heard or been taught about what a great leader in the fire service should be.

Do you believe those qualities to be weak? Make no mistake, it takes a wise, powerful, and controlled individual to not only possess those qualities, but to also exhibit them, especially in a leadership role. These are the foundational qualities you must understand and cultivate. They are also a basis for other very necessary qualities. If you can pair these attributes with courage, patience, and a healthy sense of pride, among many, you will be unstoppable.

Adopt these qualities as the foundation of your role as a leader, and you will be stunned at what you will be able to accomplish. Understanding these qualities, gaining these attributes, maintaining them, and employing them will be discussed in further detail in this book. For now, we will dive deeper into the ideas behind this method, and why they are the attributes of a strong fire officer who has the respect of their crew.

There will be a prevalent theme that I will touch upon as well throughout this book, from time to time. I will liken the crew or group of individuals you will be leading to a family, and you as their leader to the family head. Growing up, I viewed my father as a great leader. He allowed me to grow and become who I am today. He taught me many lessons. Let me fail, let me succeed. He was there to guide me, but also get out of the way when necessary. Was he perfect? No. But he was a great dad. The kind of dad that you could use words like service, sacrifice, self-control, and humility to describe.

You may have had a different experience than mine. I hope there is someone in your life that helped you in that same way. I would like you to insert that person into the spot where I use the metaphorical parent figure. Meditate on what made that person great and how they motivated you to become who you are today. What were their attributes? Do you think of that person as a leader? That person had the largest impact on your life! When they had advice, you listened. When they had a need, you went out of your way to fill it. If they gave you commendation, you felt flattered. Now imagine your crew feels the same way about you. What do you think you could accomplish?[2]

In the case of my father or any good parent, being there for their children is a battle. The battle is balancing your own needs and wants with those of your child to accomplish appropriate goals, while simultaneously displaying the right qualities and providing the highest level of care you can. Whether you are a parent or not, I'm sure we can agree that the lengths a great parent would go through to help their children succeed has no bounds.

At times, parents must "wear many hats" to accomplish all that they need to. Parents with more than one child constantly change modes and perspectives for the needs and level of understanding for each specific child. Sound like leading a crew? At the same time, the parents' workloads do not diminish, and they cannot stop caring for themselves or ignore everything else in their lives.

What you should be thinking right now is, that's a lot of work! Indeed it is, and so is leadership. View your crew as a family and yourself as the parent. You work together, train together, eat together, laugh together, go through trauma together. It's not always good times because no family is perfect. Every family has their own issues, with its members at different developmental stages, needs, wants, duties, responsibilities, etc. There are a lot of difficult scenarios to manage, but the truth is, you can do it!

Take the skill and knowledge you already possess and build upon it. Train yourself to show the right qualities, to communicate well, to create a healthy environment, and plan for success. Treat your crew like a family, show them you care about them, and you will be astounded at how far your work family will go for you, for each other, and what you will accomplish together as a team.

Take 10 minutes to meditate on this family metaphor. Think of:

- The person that had the greatest effect on your life and why.

- How you can emulate their qualities and strengths.

- How many similarities you can create between an actual family and family head with a work family and fire officer.

- Think about why exhibiting the qualities of Sacrifice, Self-control, Service, and Humility when leading others will create an unbreakable motivation and cohesion of your crew.

Chapter Two

Be Fit to Lead

You're reading this book because you want to be a better fire officer. Being better starts on the inside and starts with the inner you. Beware, if there is one thing firefighters can sniff out better than smoke, it's a phony. The person you are on the outside must reflect the person you are on the inside. Never fake the connection. Losing the respect of your crew because they believe you to be inauthentic would be devastating to your ability to lead them. What does that mean for you as a person? It means you have a lot of work to do! No matter how great you may be, there is always room for improvement. Here are the key areas you need to bolster for self-improvement:

- Your core person

- Your job knowledge

- Your ability to communicate

How to Bolster Your Core Person

Building and maintaining good qualities is a time consuming and difficult endeavor. No doubt you live a busy life, juggling your family responsibilities, work duties, maybe even a second job, etc. When there are several things vying for your limited time and energy, the process of improving upon yourself will rely heavily on how well you prioritize its importance. As an officer within your department, this is the sacrifice you signed up for. It's time to hunker down and show the world, or at least your crew and department, that you are a fire officer that deserves the brass on your collar.

A major hurtle that you may face when making the transition into a leadership role is changing the opinion others may have already made about you. The unfortunate truth is that leadership and respect start the day you're hired. From the first moment and subsequent times you have interactions with your fellow firefighters, they are creating an opinion of you and building upon it. What opinions do you believe they have formed? Do you think they thought to themselves, "Here's a future fire officer I'd love to work for?" I would venture to say that probably doesn't happen as much as we would like it to. The point is: Respect is gained over time. Have you used your time thus far within your department to gain it?

A great touchstone test would be to ask a few trusted peers, who have time and experience, their honest opinion of how the department views you. You may be pleasantly surprised, or you may have a lot of work to do. If it's the latter, that's okay. Although changing people's opinions of you is difficult, it can be done. How so?

You may have had a poor attitude in the past, you may have underperformed in a certain situation, or even had some disciplinary trouble. Whatever the case, in order to overcome preconceived notions, you must deal with those issues head on. What does that mean? It means taking responsibility! No one in the fire service wants to be around someone who cannot take responsibility for their actions, let alone work for them. Taking responsibility for your actions shows an inner and outer strength that will aid in gaining the respect you need.

Try hard to fully understand the wrong course you took, and if possible, train yourself to be better on those issues for the next time. When your peers see you strengthen your weaknesses, respect will come. There's a certain key word here that was introduced in the first chapter… Humility. Yes, it will take a heavy dose. Keep your head down, fix the problem, and remember to reevaluate your actions and yourself. Return to those you trust and see how those changes you have made were received by the department. Keep working hard, you are benefiting yourself!

In chapter 1, we discussed a few qualities you must possess to be effective as a modern fire officer. Those qualities were:

- Service

- Sacrifice

- Self-Control

- Humility

Let's examine each in turn.

The Quality of Service

Perhaps historically, you have seen that when a person is put in charge of a group of people they expect the group to serve them. They could not be more wrong, which they usually find out as their role as leader is questioned quite quickly. This is how mutinies take root! When you are in the officer role you are *serving* those under your command, not the other way around.

You are responsible for the output and product of your crew as a whole. That product is a testament to the work (service) that you put into each one of those crew members. Each crew member has different needs. You are responsible for meeting those needs and helping them to perform to the best of their abilities.

You have to get to know each crew member, not just personally, but also professionally in terms of what their specific strengths and weakness are as they pertain to their job performance. You have to prepare appropriate training for your crew and many times lead it. Sometimes, you will need to empower crew members to help others. Other times, you may just be preparing a meal for them. Whatever it is, it is a service to them. Be proud of it!

Think of how a parent serves their children. They provide a safe environment for them, feed them, teach them, care for them emotionally, take time to know them, the list is endless. This is what a parent would call the "labor of love." Meaning they *want* to do it. At the station level, you will have to *want* to provide a great service to your crew. This service can look like, feel like, and be many different things. It can be something as small as handing a Gatorade to a hard-working rookie, or as large as taking your own time on or off duty to help mentor a subordinate.

Station life resembles a family. We live together for 24-48 hours or more at a time for years. Lead that family to greatness through your service to them. When those in your crew see that as the example, they will in turn look inward, and find ways to serve the other members of their crew. The productivity of your crew will become exponential, and that crew cohesion will translate into the field.

As it turns out, service and sacrifice go hand in hand. Both play neatly off one another. What you are accomplishing is the creation of a healthy environment. As the officer this is one of your most prominent responsibilities. Whether you realize it or not, you are setting the tone or atmosphere of the station and crew with the outward example you are setting and with your verbal and non-verbal communication.

Have you been to a station or personal home before where the awkwardness is palpable in the air? Have you been to a station where you could immediately tell if it was a healthy environment or not? You, as the station officer, are responsible for curating that environment and making sure that what is palpable is the success it produces.

One of the crews on my department had a nick name for their Captain; they called him "angry dad." Their station life resembled a dysfunctional family where the kids would have to run and hide. Many times, the Captain would come to work in an irritable mood, and people would scatter to their bunks. What nick name would your crew bestow upon you? What environment are you encouraging with your behavior and example?

The Quality of Sacrifice

Time and energy are precious to all of us. They are finite and many people and responsibilities are vying for it. Although the word "sacrifice" at times may seem to insinuate the negative, the truth could not be more opposite. We sacrifice the lesser short-term want for the greater long-term need. When we trade our time and energy for something it demonstrates outwardly that it is a priority to us.

When we sacrifice time and energy for our crew, we prove to them that they are our priority. If you think that you will not have to sacrifice any extra time to your crew when you are fulfilling the role of officer, you are gravely mistaken. The time that you were able to have to yourself, whether it be in the station or even off duty, will be more limited depending on the needs of your crew. How would you view a parent that withholds their time from their children? How will your crew view you and each other if you do not prioritize them?

Understanding the needs of each of your fire-fighters takes time. Creating appropriate training takes time. Teaching that information to them, you guessed it, takes time. Never forget it is time well spent. The more time you spend on each individual, the more successful they will be. In turn, your crew will then be more successful, and in the end, you will be more successful as their leader.

I never realized just how much time and energy I would need to sacrifice to care for my crew. There are days where between running calls, cooking, training, doing chores, and tending to the issues at hand with my crew, I'm barely allowed time for a five minute break. Meanwhile, my crew had plenty of time to themselves those days. Sometimes, your crew will be enjoying a game of ping pong or goofing off some other way when you are preparing training, etc. and that's fine. They are not the officer, you are. Grow accustomed to sacrifices like that. In fact, take pride that it is your responsibility to care for them and that you are appropriately sacrificing your wants and time to do it.

The Quality of Self-Control

With service and sacrifice comes self-control. It will take a mountain of self-control to help prioritize service and sacrifice to your crew along with balancing your personal life. There are a multitude of areas we could touch on, but we will focus on a few: On and off scene, and in your personal life.

On Duty:

Have you ever been on a scene where the officer loses control? Perhaps the officer starts to scream, use profanity, etc. Did you then gain respect for that officer? Does the outcome of the scene usually become better or worse? What does that say about the officer? It says that officer does not have control over themselves. How then could they be in control of the scene?

Granted, there are many high-stress, high-risk situations we partake in as firefighters. Sometimes we must raise our voices for safety and so that commands can be heard. However, although we all have moments of loss of control, we must keep them to as close to zero as humanly possible. The respect you've built over years can be undone in moments if you cannot control yourself. People want to get behind a cool head because cool heads prevail.

Your crew needs to know that the person leading them is capable of self-control. This shows them that they can trust you to remain in control during risky situations that directly affect their livelihood. Showing self-control is even more important at the station level. Here we are in a controlled environment, the one we are creating, and we have the time to choose our verbal and nonverbal communication wisely. If we do not show control, what we are showing our crew is that we are purposely choosing to treat them poorly. Do not be an "angry dad."

<u>In Your Personal Life:</u>

You may have heard a funny twist on an old idiom that goes like this: "Tell-a-vision, Tell-a-phone, Tell-a-firefighter." Yes, as firefighters we are a big family that, for good or for worse, is in each other's business. It is a way of departmental life, therefore, the way you conduct yourself outside of work matters.

This is where self-control in our personal lives comes into play. We need to think about how we conduct ourselves off duty as well. We cannot expect our crew to change how they feel about us the moment we don an officer's uniform. Bias does not evaporate just because you are riding in the front right seat of a fire truck for the day.

If you treat friends and family poorly off duty, represent yourself foolishly in the public eye, or spend your days creating immature posts on social media, how do you think that will affect the respect you receive from your crew? When your crew looks at you, those behaviors will be in the back of their minds. Why make it harder to gain the respect of our crews by acting in those ways? Why take on more weights as we climb this mountain of leadership? Control yourself!

The Quality of Humility

The cornerstone to the above qualities that will improve your role as an officer is humility. Without it, you will find it impossible to harvest service, sacrifice, and self-control. Humility cannot be faked. Again, no one respects a phony. This quality takes the most strength to create, and the prize is worth the effort. The Bible states that "pride is before a crash" and how true that statement is. Perhaps you have had a crash predicated upon pride. Without humility, we will ignore many signs of impending doom. Understand that you do not know everything and will never know everything. The day you stop learning is the most dangerous day of your career.

Humility will allow you to look inward and understand your limitations and weaknesses. It will allow you to take criticism whether it is given tastefully or not. It will allow you to take responsibility for your mistakes and learn from them. It will allow you to see that each member of your crew has something to teach you and add to the overall product your crew creates.

Humble officers are approachable. Humble officers work hard around the station, even doing menial tasks such as cleaning and cooking. Humble officers do not ignore warning signs or "red flags." They will not believe they are above the danger and take those warnings into account as the danger approach. Humble officers understand that when a crew excels the commendation goes to the crew; and when the crew falls short the blame rests upon the officer's shoulders. You are a shield to your crew made possible by your humble attitude. Work hard to cultivate this important trait, and you will see just how motivational it truly is.

There are times when a parent errs. That parent shows humility by apologizing and discussing it with their children. The parent allows themselves to grow from the incident and treat the child better when the same situation occurs again. In the same way, we as officers are not infallible and must show that we can apologize and remain in control when necessary. When we put what we say into practice, respect will follow.

Do not allow your humility to be confused with a lack of firmness. At times those on your crew may question your leadership, essentially testing your limits. These situations cannot be ignored. Proper boundaries can be set and held while remaining humble. Chapter 3 will develop this thought further.

The qualities we've discussed thus far are a solid foundation on your journey to becoming a great modern fire officer. I challenge you to go further. Take a deep dive into yourself. The greater you can become internally, the greater the external effect will be.

For further reading on bettering yourself and congruent leadership ideals, I recommend reading the following sources:

- Jordan Peterson, *12 Rules for Life,* Penguin 2019. Here you will find a guided meditation of the self. The author delves into creating a better you with a thoughtful look at biology, sociology, and psychology.

- Simon Sinek, *Leaders Eat Last,* Portfolio 2017. Mr. Sinek has very similar ideas to the ones found here. Although tailored to private enterprise, there is much to be gained by his perspective.

- Jocko Willink & Leif Babin, *Extreme Ownership,* St. Martin's Press 2017. From their leadership roles on battle grounds in Iraq, the authors adapt hard lessons learned to build efficient teams in the corporate world.

If and when you read these references, meditate on the way their guidance can translate to your role as an officer. Put into action every idea and recommendation that would bolster you as a leader and add to the overall health of your crew. Ponder how to put those ideas into action at the station level.

How to Bolster Your Job Knowledge

In order to qualify for the position of officer within your department, a certain number of prerequisites set out by your administration were met. This is a basic body of knowledge you must possess, most likely it is the minimum requirement necessary to function in that capacity. If you are new to the position, you have a lot to learn! Do not let that destroy your motivation to continue. It is exciting to think that there is so much more depth to the job that you fell in love with! Do not let that love cool off.

How do you create the most extensive knowledge base possible? Treat everything as a learning experience. Even the most mundane of calls can teach you something new. On the job training starts the day you are hired. Hopefully you have been paying attention and learning since day one.

Most likely you have had to fulfill different ranks and tasks as you made your way to an officer position. Have you tried to truly master those past positions to the best of your ability? When someone in those positions you have previously fulfilled ran into an obstacle or problem, did they call you for insight? It is very important for you to not only have fulfilled the roles of your subordinates, but for you to also know those roles well. As the officer, your crew will be looking to you for guidance. Although you will not always have the answer, being prepared with many insightful answers will show your crew that you can understand their position and have true empathy for their situation.

Learn Everything

What we do as firefighters has no bounds, especially if we are also paramedics. I have been everything from a dog walker to a plumber, to command of major hazardous material incidents, and everything in between. I'm not trying to wow you with my experiences but make it clear that we are called upon to do anything and everything by our communities. The citizens of your area call their emergency number when they are desperate for help. This does not always mean it is a fire or a medical emergency. Being open to learning as many skills as possible will allow you to be useful on the call at 3am when the pipe breaks at the elderly couples' home and they don't know what to do.

There seems to be no limit to the possibilities of what the community may ask us to do. You need to know what to do, or at the very least have a general idea of how to help. We also need to know who to turn to in as many areas as possible. Know what resources you have available to you on your immediate crew. Perhaps one of them has the skills necessary to safely mitigate the issue, or at least give some helpful guidance. Obviously, we have limitations as set out by our department for what we can attempt in the field, but that does not mean we cannot go beyond our normal call of duty in a healthy way when the opportunity presents itself.

Expand Your Awareness Level

Have at least a basic understanding or "awareness level" of different special operations. Hazardous materials, confined space, trench rescue, high angle rescue, low angle rescue, dive rescue, etc. You cannot be a master of all these disciplines, however, having at least an acute awareness of what could be a possible call you may run into will give you an edge. That edge equals *safety.*

When you pair your knowledge and awareness with the skill set of your crew, you can gauge whether your crew can safely handle the incident and/or call with their capabilities and the resources they have on hand. Showing your crew that you are knowledgeable in a great range of areas pertaining to their safety, along with the ability to mitigate a variety of emergencies, creates trust in you. Asking for help (humility) when necessary, shows strength and wisdom.

Learn to Teach

Be an available source! Those that teach well have a firm grasp on the content at hand. Being an available resource and instructor will give you respect from your crew and more knowledge. Get involved with your training division to possibly instruct training on behalf of the department. If you do, choose a subject that is weak for you. This will give you the motive and urgency to become very proficient in that subject matter.

If you have a mentor, get their feedback on training that was pivotal for them, and training that they believe can be pivotal for you. If possible, take advantage of national training programs, classes, and expos. Although not all the ideas found there may apply to your jurisdiction, you will no doubt have a fresh outlook and greater knowledge base.

How to Bolster Your Communication Skills

As you move further up the hierarchical ladder in your fire organization, the more you will be performing physical skills less and communicating more. In fact, get ready to communicate more than you ever have before. If you are more of an introverted person, you may have been able to get away with a limited amount of personal interaction thus far. That is over! You must interact with each member of your crew throughout the day every shift and many times off duty as well.

Communication and public speaking are usually not what most people would call their strengths. In fact, on average people are just as afraid of public speaking as death, corruption, or snakes![1] This is definitely not a fear or weakness you as an officer can afford to have. The hard truth is that as an officer you will have many difficult and emotionally draining conversations. The time to practice your communication and delivery is not last minute on calls or during emotionally charged conversations, but with trusted friends and mentors. If you are called upon to speak in front of a group of bystanders or calm a family group and inform them that their loved one has passed away, are you ready?

How can you overcome weakness in this area? More learning. There are four basic forms of communication: verbal, non-verbal, written, and visual. Verbal, written, and visual are very self-explanatory and are usually more easily understood. The black sheep of the family and hardest one to master is non-verbal communication.[2] In fact, it is thought that 55% or more of all conversational communication is non-verbal.

Non-verbal communication is a very nuanced form of communication that can have very different meanings across different peoples, age groups, and ethnicities. Your non-verbal communication skills are essential to good firehouse communication. Your facial expressions, the posture you choose, whether you cross your arms or not, if your feet are facing the person or turned away, your eye contact, etc., all have implications about how you are feeling and if you are open to what the other person is saying.

In your career as an officer, you will do each of those basic forms of communication multiple times and sometimes simultaneously. Your communication ability is the glue that binds your crew, the citizens, and your administration together. The conversations you have, the emails you send, the instructions and commands you give, and your contact with the community, is a balancing act and you are the conductor of the show.

Perhaps one of the most important forms of communication not usually included in the basic forms is listening. The wise listen first, collect their thoughts, and then speak. Gather as much information from the sender as you can by listening to and assessing the many forms of communication that person is sending. When you have understood or "received" that person or "senders" message in full, you then "know your audience" and have an amazing foundation to truly reach that person as you communicate with them.

When communication like this takes place, that person will feel validated and understood, they will not be on the defensive and will be more open to new ideas and change. If you can truly harness this skill, not only will your ability to communicate skyrocket, but it will also put you and those you communicate with at ease even during the most difficult conversations.

When I was reaching out to become an officer, I was under the impression that 90% of the work would be action, like running calls and directing emergency operations. The other 10% would be station duties, communication, etc. I've come to realize that to be successful, 90% of the work I do is communication and everything else makes up the 10%. My point is, to be a great officer you must be a great communicator. To be a great communicator you must be a great listener, be humble, and available. Get ready to listen and converse more than you ever have before! Firefighters that feel understood and have their expectations clearly communicated to them, no matter the difficulty, will thrive. They will be the firefighters who leave the firehouse with a smile.

For further reading on improving your communication skills, I recommend the following sources.

- Joseph Grenny, Kerry Patterson, Ron McMillan, Al Switzler, & Emily Gregory, *Crucial Conversations: Tools for Talking When Stakes are High,* McGraw Hill, 3rd Edition, 2021.

- Allan & Barbara Pease, *The Definitive Book of Body Language*, Bantam 2006.

Being fit to lead is like a beautiful clock with many intricate working parts. When put together with skill and care, it is something that with attentive maintenance can last far into the future and be appreciated with time. Whether you are a long-time officer or not, truly reflect upon yourself. Be honest with yourself. Make a list of what you believe your strengths and limitations to be and improve upon them. Reach out to a mentor or your closest confidants as you improve to see if you are on the right track. Get excited for the possibility to better yourself. The charisma surrounding you will be hard to ignore.

Chapter Three

Creating a Healthy Firehouse Environment

Would you expect a child that has a poor home life to exceed at school and have no social problems? Would it be right for the parents of that household to expect high grades and good behavior when they do not provide a safe and caring environment for their children? Although some children may be able to deal with such conditions and still thrive, why make them overcome that in the first place? How much better could they have been without those hurdles?

In the same way, we cannot expect our crew to thrive in less-than-ideal circumstances. Why should we expect a great work ethic and work product if we do not do our part to create the environment necessary for success? How do we lead instead of hinder? This chapter will explore some suggestions to help.

Lead by Example

We cannot expect something of others we lead without first doing it ourselves. We cannot create a healthy environment if it is built on hypocrisy. It must be "do as I say *and* as I do." Leading by example takes serious conscious effort. One of the hardest things for humans to do is to control our emotions. There are many times when we may feel a certain way about a topic or have a strong emotion, but revealing that attitude to the crew could undo a lot of work we have done to gain their respect. Just as a parent is cautious to behave or communicate in a certain way around their children to preserve the bond of trust that they have built with them, you must control yourself for the sake of your crew.

Leading by example goes much further than controlling our outward expressions. We have to show our crew that we care about them and create an environment in which they can flourish. Children flourish in environments where clear expectations for, and examples of, behaviors are set.[1] Would a good parent look to the children to clean up after them? Do they believe the needs and wants of the children to be beneath them or treat them like indentured servants? No, they understand that although they are in charge, the child's needs come first.

You are not worth more than any member of your crew. In fact, you should hold each member's needs above the needs of your own. Show this to them by your actions. What do your current actions reveal about you? When your actions show you place your crew on a pedestal, this creates trust within your crew and a safe place for them to excel.

You as the officer must be the gold standard for what is expected at the station level in as many areas as you can. This is where possessing the qualities in the previous chapter will help you to succeed, especially humility. Don't be afraid to get your hands dirty. Something as simple as finishing up one of your crew mate's laundry while they are out on a call goes a long way. Yes, we are busy as officers, but we must show that we are never too busy or unconcerned about our crew.

If your crew sees you working hard for them, even at the most menial tasks while taking *pride* in what you are doing, it will not be ignored for long. Pride like that is contagious. Your crew will see your example and emulate it. In time, they will start to emulate all your examples. Your crew will find ways to not only follow your example but *be* an example to others within the firehouse. Let your example help your fire-fighters pair pride with their personal work output, no matter how insignificant the task. Commend them on the work they have accomplished and applaud them for their efforts.

Be Fair

Do not allow any room for impartiality. Unfortunately, it is human nature to be more friendly toward individuals who have certain attributes that you find more endearing. Your leadership cannot be monochromatic. So much more can be learned and enjoyed from the people you're most different from. Just as parents celebrate the similarities and differences of their children, we must do the same with our crew. Never play favorites.

Historically, many warring nations used partiality to conquer their foes. The Romans were particularly well versed at this, in what they called "*divide et impera*," or as we usually refer to it "divide and conquer." Allow your firehouse to be divided and it will be conquered. Conquered by unhealthy practices and attitudes toward each other, your department, and the public. Instead of being a divider through partiality, be a uniter through the equal treatment you show to each of your crew members.

Never allow factions to form between the members of your crew, much less blossom into a division. Discourage behavior that breeds division immediately. The root word of discourage is courage, and it will take just that to make a stand for peace. When a group of people live together, divisiveness can take many forms and happen often. Whatever form it takes, use your departmental policies and communication abilities to extinguish it before it does further damage.

Be Positive

If there is one thing that is a stake through the heart of a healthy crew, it's negativity. Negativity is a cancer that will go from benign to fatal rather aggressively if left unchecked. Just like cancer, it must be addressed in its infancy and removed immediately. How do we prepare for and extract this killer attitude even if it is well established? Constant perspective realignment.

Perspective realignment starts with you as the officer. You cannot allow yourself to be negative. Just as you would protect yourself from the dangers of physical cancers with regular checkups, you must do regular self-examinations for negativity. When you find an area where you are inclined towards negativity you must cut it out by realigning your perspective.

Reflecting on the opportunities and successes you have enjoyed throughout your career and life will help with this self-check practice. Make a list of the positive experiences you have had and the differences you have made in your department, no matter how small. Meditate on all those positive changes. Let those experiences help you to overcome the negativity you have by replacing negative feelings with positive ones.

You usually find what you set out to look for, so if you are looking for negatives you will find them. Train yourself to look for positives instead. When your crew responds negatively, usually to change, do not join in. Refocus their attention onto the ways that change can make things better. Remind them of the positives that they do enjoy.

In my experience, the times when feelings of negativity arise are often around the dinner table, which is family time. As firefighters, we prepare our own family style meals, and we eat well. There is usually an evident level of pride put into preparing a meal for our fellow crew mates. If the mealtime conversation trends toward the negative, I love redirecting the crew's attention to the fact that we get paid to prepare and eat a delicious meal together. It's hard to deny the perks that are rare outside of the fire department. We have many reasons for positivity in our careers. Keep your crew's perspective guided toward the positives and away from negative thinking.

Be Available

It is very hard to build and maintain a healthy crew environment if you are absent. Being available and accessible to your crew is paramount. How well can you manage a crew and understand their needs and wants from your bunk room or locked office? Don't be a dead-beat parent and only show up for the major events. Be around for as many of the minor ones as well.

Helping to check out equipment or do station chores that are not your responsibility is a perfect way to show you are available and care. This is a great time to assess the crew's health and work ethic as well. When you are an integral part of the daily routine, you are easily accessible, and the right kind of conversations can flow.

When you are working in your office, have an "open door policy" when possible by welcoming your firefighters to stop by. This demonstrates that even issues the crew may perceive as minor are still important to you. How you handle your body language also signals to your crew your level of availability and readiness to communicate. Be cognizant of holding yourself in an "open" posture and not a "closed off" posture.

If you are hunched over, eyes down, or arms crossed (closed posture) you are sending the signal that now is not a good time to communicate. An open posture consists of keeping your back straight, eyes up, and arms open. An open posture gives the impression that you are available and ready to listen. These postures are an outward expression of our subconscious, so it takes a lot of body and spatial awareness to maintain a posture that shows availability.

Have Balance

The average firefighter works for 24 hours or more at a time. That entire time cannot and should not be constituted of work only. A healthy amount of down time (that does not include mealtime) must be allowed for during the shift. Private time and group activities are an essential part of creating a healthy workplace environment.[2] How can you balance all the activities of the day?

It starts with understanding each of your crew members. If your crew is younger, less experienced, and in need of training or more supervision, you may be allowing for less leisure than you would for a more experienced crew. Whatever the allotted time is, make it known to the crew. Let them know they will have time to themselves. This will allow them to find a healthier state of mind when it comes to learning and working in high stress scenarios.

In my experience there are two main ways fire crews build camaraderie – under stress and without. Putting your training to work on emergency scenes and helping the public in the face of danger brings us together as a team. However, it does so in an environment under which we are burdened by a large amount of stress and may come away with unsettling memories. Having the opportunity to build our teamwork and trust at the station level without stress is essential. It creates a team in a controlled environment free from unneeded stress and intensity. When we come together in a stress-free environment we can perform even better when under great stress.

The armed forces take this approach with recruits. The recruits undergo many team building exercises

where the group must work together to overcome
preset obstacles. The obstacles are impossible to
pass alone. This allows for, and forces the group, to
forge a uniting bond to trust each other while working together before they are taking live fire from an
enemy.[3]

A great way to include healthy crew leisure time
is with team sports. Firefighters love competition.
Healthy team competitions will help your crew work
together, allow them to exercise and blow off steam.[4]
Follow department guidelines for use of time and
safety, and make sure you are a part of the festivities.
Tell each member of the crew that you would personally like them to join and have a part in the game.

In my career, we have gone through many sports
– basketball, ping pong, football, swimming, pickle
ball, wiffle ball, etc. In my opinion, nothing can bring
my crews together and forge stronger bonds at the
station level than playing sports together. We created
a solid team *before* we were put in harm's way and
under stress.

Again, proper balance here is key. Playing games
all day and ignoring necessary duties and training
will end in a lack of respect of your crew within the
department, as well as for you as their officer. With
discretion however, allowing just the right amount
of proper leisure time for crew building activities

will create an environment that will produce happy hard-working firefighters that perform their duties well *together*.

Have Clear Boundaries

A common part of interacting with your environment is testing its limits. With children, the study of psychology that deals with this issue literally calls it "limit testing."[5] In a nutshell, the child is finding the edge of their care taker's authority. The child usually tests the unspoken rules of the home to see where the parents draw a hard line, many times without realizing they're even doing it. Unfortunately, limit exploration is usually not a comfortable process for any parties involved. How will the parent deal with this behavior?

The parent must handle the issue in a timely, straightforward manner with clear reasoning. The parent must also explain the possible repercussions if that behavior is continued. If the parent can employ that method with patience and in a setting that will not embarrass the child or put them on the defense, many times that behavior will cease.

Adults test the limits of others as well, although in a much more sophisticated and conscious way, and sometimes in a negative fashion. When limits are explored in a negative way that strikes the edge of what is considered acceptable, it cannot be ignored. You must help that person to understand where the edge of that limit was, and clearly communicate the repercussions of continuing past it.

As an officer, you cannot allow your crew to undermine you or for you to be "stepped on." Your crew from time- to-time will test the limits of your authority and established practices. Sometimes, it is done unknowingly and other times with ill intent. Whichever the situation or intent, an appropriate amount of timely communication must take place in order for both parties to understand the limit that was tested, and how/why the behavior cannot continue. When applicable do this in a private setting and be honest, open, and firm. Be straightforward and specific on the disciplinary action that will be taken if the behavior were to continue, and promptly follow through with the discussed discipline if it happens again.

When I first became a Captain within my department, I inherited a senior crew that I was close with and had worked with many times before. In fact, the driver engineer for my truck was one of the driver engineers that taught and helped me to get promoted to that position previously. I was very excited to have him as a driver, the first shift, however, proved to be a lot different than what I was expecting. That driver was clearly chaffed that I was now his officer. His body language and verbal ques made it known that he had little interest in respecting my decision making. Obviously, this was a test of the boundaries between us whether he was aware of it or not.

I could not allow this attitude to continue. I spoke with him privately and told him that I was extremely excited to have him as a resource on the crew and thanked him for his previous help with my career. I was straightforward with him and told him that I noticed he was having trouble respecting my decision making and asked him what I could do to change that. I asked him to put himself in my position, what he would do in my position, and if he would allow an attitude like that to continue.

I made it clear that I could not let it continue and risk losing the respect of the rest of my crew. In this instance, he did not even realize what he was doing and apologized. I reassured him again that I respected him, was acutely aware of his abilities, and appreciated the level of experience he brought to the team. I asked him to help me with my new role as Captain and to help one of the firefighters on our crew with becoming a driver engineer. After this conversation, the tension was gone, and the difference was obvious. Our crew became closer.

You never know when or where a boundary will be tested, but when it does act in a timely manner. Speak with that person in a calm, controlled voice. Spell out the issue as clearly as possible and discuss it together. Make it known that that behavior cannot continue. Validate that person's place within the department and their strengths. Empower them to expend their energy in a way that brings the crew together instead of pulling it apart.

When you take a hard stand for what is important to you, your crew and the department will notice. The warning message will be received, and it will be unlikely that you will have to have that same conversation twice or take similar actions again.

No one wants to play guessing games with their career and life. Make sure each member of your crew understands the proper limits and boundaries you expect of them. Transparency with expectations is an integral piece to maintaining a healthy firehouse environment.

Chapter Four

Plan for Success

If you want your crew to be successful, you must first understand what that means to each crew member, the crew as a whole, the department, and you as their officer. Envision what this looks like for your crew and the work product you want produced. What is the best level of service you can perceive that is attainable? What areas must you personally fortify first before taking on this endeavor? What are the strengths and weaknesses of each crew member? What special disciplines must be addressed? This is obviously a major fact-finding mission that must be approached honestly. It also must be approached as a *team.*

Get Everyone Involved

This is a perfect time for healthy inclusive crew communication. Speak with your crew, share your intentions and vision. Explain to them how and why attaining that vision will improve not just their work lives, but also their home lives. Have your crew brainstorm ideas as well. Help the crew to become a think tank on ways to improve. Encourage openness, honesty, and constructive criticism.

Encourage your firefighters to analyze their current methods and find ideas that will improve those methods at the station level and on the street. While your crew is finding ways to improve, observe them individually to see where you can help improve them as firefighters. Set a time to discuss the ideas that are generated together as a crew, so each one can sharpen the ideas of the other.

Be an example of how to share your ideas and positive criticism. Humility here will go a long way. Review the ways you believe you as the officer can improve and how you plan on making the needed changes. Invite honest and respectful feedback from your crew. Approaching the conversation this way will lower any sense of defense anyone may be having, and a more honest and healthy conversation will follow.

Make Worthwhile Goals

Whatever way you choose to find what goals are important to your crew individually or as a whole, write them down and be specific. Make sure the goals are attainable with the resources you have access to. Consider using the SMART method for achieving your goals. This means that a goal must be Specific, Measurable, Achievable, Relevant, and Time-Bound.[1] This is a tried-and-true recipe for finding successful goals. It weeds out the goals that may need to be shelved for a later time or set aside all together. This is of course not the only way to determine appropriate goals. Find and use a method that works for you.

Once you have a list of attainable goals, you can prioritize them in an order that makes sense. Not every goal is one that takes months or years to accomplish. It may be as simple as passing on the station to the next crew in better order, or something else that can be started immediately. Some goals may be foundational, meaning they need to be accomplished first to set up the next one. Just as you would build a home from the ground up, so too will goals need to be skillfully ordered so that they build upon each other and make sense.

Create Timelines

Each goal has its own timeline to complete and must be juggled along with the others. Some building stages of a home can be done simultaneously, others paused until a more important step is complete or, at times, need to be rebuilt the correct way. Each goal can be likened to the above.

All of the goals set can be difficult to handle and track, especially the larger the crew. Communicate the plan and use your crew to help you stay on track. Let them know what you as a team are currently working on and provide feedback on the process. Don't forget your crew's feedback as well.

Maintaining progress and making it enjoyable takes a lot of preparation on your part, which also takes place on different timelines. I like to prepare myself in increments: before each shift, for each week, for each month, ahead three months, and ahead six months. If you use this type of future planning, you can plug in the goals you have in their appropriate time positions.

Again, be realistic about the time needed to finish a goal, especially when it involves multiple people.

Something as simple as a quick tabletop training can be planned for a single shift ahead of time. However, completing a state hazardous materials course could take up to 160 hours or more to complete and should be set to a target of three to six months on the low end.

Your timeline does not have to be set in stone. In fact, allowing some fluidity is necessary and will minimize discouragement from the inability to complete the goal in time. You may be able to move some goals ahead of schedule or others back, and that's okay. Communicate the ups and downs of the process to the crew or individual it deals with specifically, brainstorm with them the best way forward, and make it happen.

Stay on Course

Maintaining the goals and timelines you create does not have to be an intensely time-consuming endeavor. For example, planning for the next shift may only take a few minutes but the payoff will be noticeable. Taking time to review the roster, and reflect on the personnel on duty, will allow you to prepare for their specific needs and the resources available to meet them. Look back on the timeline you've created, check off the completions, update your current

completion levels, and adjust the end points accord-
ingly. Share the progress with your crew and evalu-
ate it together. If there is a crew member that is not
abreast of the plan or only at your station for the day,
inform them of what your crew is trying to accomplish and invite them to take part.

Do not train just to train. Busy work will kill your
team's drive. No one wants to work hard on something with little to no value and feel like their time is
being wasted. Ensure that whatever training you are
preparing is necessary and realistic. Also consider ex-
tenuating circumstances. Continuing training on certain days may not be appropriate due to a personal
issue of one of your crew mates or even sheer call
volume.

Training does not have to happen every single day,
there is no need to force it. Let it happen organically,
when appropriate, and when the crew has the proper
amount of energy. Forcing your plan on your crew
when they are tired, haven't eaten, etc. will result in
mutiny. And rightly so! Keep all their circumstances
in mind to keep your plan healthy and the crew will
invest in it too.

As a marine captain must constantly make minute
adjustments to the helm to keep the ship on course,
so too must you be aware of fine tuning the course
of your crew. Do not wait until you are off heading to

correct the direction of travel. Do not be nitpicky, focus on issues that will have a real chance of hindering your goals or that may fail to meet expectations.

If you have been generous with commendation, when there is a need for a slight adjustment, it will not feel like the only time you are communicating is to criticize. So, kill your crew with kindness. Most likely, they deserve every bit of it for the many things they do during the day. When tactful criticism is needed, it will be accepted much more readily. This will be discussed in greater detail in Chapter 8.

Plans Change

Keep any changes to expectations clear. As an officer this entails a lot of listening, conversing, and re-evaluating. No one can read your mind. Expectations are sometimes confused with assumptions. Assumptions can often end poorly. Do not allow room for a poor outcome. You are the leader; the poor outcome is a testament to you.

Instead, collect your thoughts. Give clear directions, and make sure the message is received and understood. Take time explaining exactly what you would like the outcome to be and *why*. Knowing why is a powerful tool. If your crew doesn't know why they are doing something and understand its purpose, they will not become invested in accomplishing the task.

A great time to inject when expectations are met well or could be improved upon is after a call. In my experience, the crew always has at least a quick conversation, if not more, about the last call we ran together. This may take place in the fire apparatus, at the station, or both. Let them know how well they did, and address some of the weaknesses, if there were any worth addressing.

This is also a good time to communicate some of the ways *you* could have done a better job. Ask them if they have any recommendations or ideas to make the service provided better, or in a safer manner. Remember, focus on what matters. Some issues most likely will be an isolated event or not even worth addressing. Be careful to never embarrass anyone for what has taken place on or off of an emergency scene. Never hold back appreciation for a job well done and make it constant!

Chapter Five

Trust & Empowerment

Have you ever had a superior who interject-ed his/her style, opinion, or method of doing something every chance they had? How did that way of management affect your performance or the per-formance of the team? Most likely, it robbed the crew of efficiency and satisfaction in anything they did. I feel there are few people who long to be microman-aged, and for good reason!

When you micromanage, you are sending the mes-sage to your subordinates that you believe they are under qualified. No one wants to be treated as if they have no idea what they are doing. Especially professional and experienced firefighters. You as the officer are ultimately responsible for their training. If you do not trust them to perform their skills, you are making it clear that you have failed to train them.

Stop Micromanagement

Forcing a person to do a skill or action your way, even if it is better, will never be as efficient as allowing the person to demonstrate that skill as they have learned it and practiced it in that moment. Micromanaging your firefighters on scene gives on-lookers the impression the person attempting the skill is unprepared. To give that impression to others about your crew among many things is disrespectful.

Do not confuse micromanagement with training that we facilitate on emergency calls, like aiding a new paramedic in their first intubation attempt. Training like that is not micromanagement because it has been communicated and agreed upon beforehand. When there is a need for training, because of poor technique, address it tactfully after the call.

Micromanagement alienates crew members and does not allow them to take pride in their work. If you have a paintbrush in your hand and a painter is behind you facilitating the movement of the brush, did you paint the picture? How proud can you be of a painting like that? Let your team work without you trying to interfere in every movement. Fighting the urge to micromanage takes trust. How can we learn to trust our crew members?

Trust

Before you can learn to trust your crew members, you must learn to trust yourself. Micromanagement is a clear sign that you do not trust your leadership abilities. At its core, the main reason most "leaders" tend towards micromanagement is so that they can feel in control. Officers who are not well prepared will feel out of control in the station and on the street. Instead of becoming better prepared through training, communication, etc. the unprepared officer will then attempt to manage every detail to form fit the limited way they do know, and voila, micromanagement.

A strong leader puts in the hard, time-consuming work, to understand their crew members' abilities and then has faith in their own leadership to allow those crew members to showcase their skills without interference. The faith mentioned above is not a blind faith. Again, it comes from trust, which you can build from employing all the methods thus far that we have discussed in this book and will discuss from mentors and from experience. Once you have learned to trust yourself, then you can learn to trust your crew to be more autonomous.

Early on in my officer career, I inherited a crew that was subjected regularly to micromanagement. It was so bad that they would check with me before even doing the most basic skills like taking a blood pressure on a medical call. These firefighters were not new to the job and because of the micromanagement they had dealt with they were not very motivated.

Through my knowledge of them and my observances, I knew they had the skill sets needed to be able to work on their own with minimal direction. I communicated to them that I trusted their abilities, they did not have to check with me for every minor detail, and I did not want them to feel bound to my way of doing things. I made it clear to them that the most important outcome was the one where we are efficient, helpful, and safe, and we agreed there are many ways to get there. I informed them that if something was important, I would tell them, otherwise I wanted them to perform the skills they learned *their* way.

Because of the trust I gave them, our crew became extremely efficient. They were motivated to showcase *their* way of doing things. This allowed them to take pride in the product they were creating, and in themselves. That pride became contagious and spread to other aspects of their work as well, on and off calls. At the same time, I learned better ways of giving care and mitigating emergencies from their examples. I then gave them positive feedback on the great work they were doing. Our crew dynamic and output improved synergistically.

The proof was there for all to see; allow your crew to do their job and they will surprise you. Even new recruits with limited experience can still bring something to the table. I've learned a lot from probationary employees and crew members with a small amount of time within the department. Many times, they are hungry for new information and skills, and know new methods you were not aware of. You will be surprised to see what they can do when you make a safe place for them to display what they've learned.

Never be Negative

Another killer of trust and productivity is negative motivation. The very use of negative motivation proves in itself that trust is not there. Negative motivation is the act of threatening an employee with discipline or some other undesirable outcome if their work is not up to a certain standard, which is often ambiguous. No one can be successful under the fear of the unknown over a career.

Nothing will plateau your crew's work output faster than a constant fear of possible consequences. Your crew will not focus on going above and beyond, because this adds to the amount of exposure they will have to possible repercussions. As a result, they will instead do the bare minimum. When our crews do not believe we trust them to make the right decisions especially in the "gray areas" of our jobs, they will never rise to the occasion for sake of self-preservation. They will never be able to gain a heightened sense of pride in their work, and work ethic will dwindle.

Pressure is not always a negative motivator. In our line of work, we constantly come under pressure. From dealing with a cardiac event in front of the patients' loved ones, to extricating a victim of a vehicle accident in front of a group of bystanders with camera phones. There will always be a level of pressure every time the bell or tones ring for an emergency event.

Firefighters must be prepared and accustomed to working in high-pressure environments. However, not all pressure is created equally or necessary in an already stressful occupation. We need to be aware of how we use pressure to motivate the crew. Healthy pressure, if indicated, is always used in conjunction with other teaching methods and positive criticism. For example, if you had a firefighter who required motivation in achieving a faster time to donning their bunker gear, what do you think would motivate them not only in the short-term but in the long-term as well?

A. Single that firefighter out unannounced and time their bunk out time in front of the crew.

B. Announce to the crew that you will be having a bunk out competition the next shift, where the crew will have to try to beat your time and provide advice on how to make their times faster.

In both instances there is a level of pressure that will be put on that firefighter to attain the fastest time that they can manage. The (A) example is a form of negative pressure due to the fear of embarrassment in front of their fellow firefighters and lack of an adjacent teaching method. The (B) example shows a form of positive peer pressure from friendly competition with training and time to practice.

Which method of pressure do you think will keep that firefighter motivated to retain a faster bunker gear donning time? Find every way you can to replace negative pressure with positive pressure. Remember, to be positive, the pressure must come with clear communication, training, and constructive feedback.

Empower

Instead of threatening our crew with consequences and negative pressure, we need to empower them with the right principles and training. Empowering someone means that you are giving them the authority to act with their own expertise. When they can do this, it creates a "buy in" that will make that person want to work harder. That firefighter will feel valued because they made a personal difference in the product the crew created, and rightly so. Feeling valued is a powerful motivator. It is your job to give them the expertise to be trustworthy and the opportunities to feel valued.

Again, this takes serious work and observational awareness on your part. You must know the strengths and weaknesses of your individual firefighters and the crew. Focus on building up the weaknesses you find as it will bolster their strengths, resulting in a large net improvement. In the areas you know to be a certain individual's or crew's strength, empower them to act using those strengths. Most likely you will be amazed at what that crew or firefighter can accomplish.

In the off chance that they do not knock it out of the park, that's okay, it does not have to be perfect.

Real learning comes from dealing with our failures. Nothing is as persistent as a memory of a failure. If we encourage them to try and try again while fortifying the weaknesses with training, the failure will be overcome in a big way, and will rarely, if ever, be repeated.

The Next Level

Do not be closed off to welcoming new ideas for strategies and tactics from your crew. This can even happen on a fire scene with prior station level communication and agreed upon expectations. Make it known to your crew that you are open to ideas of how a call could go better. Just as you would want a crew member to voice a safety concern, you should also want them to voice a strategy and tactic that may be the better route of attack. This, however, is a delicate balance that comes with communicated boundaries and a trust that is built by employing the tactics learned so far in this book.

You as an officer gain your crew's trust by showing them you can lead your crew to a safe and favorable outcome on emergency calls. You show trust in your crew by fielding appropriate recommendations when facing a challenge, and then applying that recommendation when it provides a better outcome for all. Now, put the two together.

Lead the crew in a calm and respectful discussion of the best course of action during a stressful incident when the situation justifies it. Your crew will trust your judgment in the course of action chosen and get to work enthusiastically. They will do this because you are leading them as an empowered team. The level of trust and cohesion gained in these moments will forge a team bond unlikely to fail in the most difficult of trials. This robust form of collaboration is at the heart of the healthiest crews.

Empowerment is not confined to a one-on-one, officer to subordinate or officer to crew relationship. Empowerment can take many forms and should be approached as a team or crew. Empowerment can come from an informal leader, like a senior firefighter or driver engineer to a less senior firefighter. It can also come from a probationary firefighter who is tasked with table topping an educational discussion. There are many examples. You as the officer want empowerment to take place on as many levels as possible between every member of your crew. The more it happens the more conducive the environment is for learning, living, working, and meeting goals.

Empowerment Means Being a Mentor

Mentorship is one of the most life altering, career changing gifts you can give to the members of your crew and fire department. Don't wait for someone to come to you. Seek out anyone who wants to better themselves or who you believe has potential. Help them to become the best version of themselves within the fire department. Impart to them the lessons you have learned on leadership and the important ways in which they can improve. Take time to help them set goals to reach their target.

Many municipalities allow firefighters to "step up" into the role of a promoted position. With a certain amount of training and certifications, they are allowed to fulfill a role when there is a vacancy of that promoted position. If that is true for your department, help everyone you can to reach up and learn the positions above them. There will never be a better firefighter than one who understands the positions above and around them by fulfilling them personally and proficiently.

Being a mentor is a sacrifice, but in turn it will make you a better leader. When you teach others, it forces you to learn and stay as current as possible in all aspects of your field. Some of my most prideful moments have not come from showcasing my own skills on a call or even receiving an award within the department. It has come from helping others succeed and enjoying how it has positively affected their lives, the department, and the respect I have gained. I challenge you to do the same.

If the parents of a child do not allow the child to make decisions, how do you think that child will develop? How would they stack up to their peers when facing challenges? Learning to make decisions in controlled environments is key to a child's development. It will give them the ability to grow and make decisions that are increasingly harder. A parent that fails to train a child to make decisions is doing that child a major injustice. When that child is not part of the family's decision-making process, they become disillusioned, disinterested, mediocre, and feel undervalued.

Many times, children like that may never leave the home and become dependent when they become adults because of their inabilities. This situation where the child becomes a dependent adult is commonly referred to as a "failure to launch." A child must be empowered to grow to become a healthy independent adult. In the same way, your fire family must be empowered to be a part of the decision-making processes. You must hone their skills and value their opinions. They must be empowered to grow within the department. You would never want to be responsible for a crew of firefighters stuck on the launching pad. Search out ways to help their careers lift off.

Chapter Six

Overcoming Fear

What we've discussed so far within these pages is no small task. It takes concentrated time and energy and does not magically happen overnight. It is directly correlated to the efforts you make. You may feel overwhelmed if you look up half-way through the climb and see the top of the mountain is still far above. Even when you reflect on the goals you've achieved, you may feel there are so many more to go, and fear can creep in.

As an officer, if you have, or have had, feelings of inadequacy you are not alone. Feeling that way is normal, you are normal. The truth is no one is perfect, you are not perfect, your crew is not perfect, and neither am I. Although you know that, don't forget it. It's a healthy perspective to maintain, not just for you but for those around you as well. Do not hold others to a standard you would not want to be held to and hopefully they will return the favor.

Be quick to forgive others and hopefully they will be quick to forgive you. Remember, forgive yourself. Creating an environment like this will ease the feelings of inadequacy and help foster progression past the stagnation fear may cause. Pair that nourishing environment with sheer determination. Make your goals known to your mentor, your crew, or someone important to you. Let them cheer you on in your journey and fight alongside you.

It has taken me years and much trial and error to build on and create concepts that helped me stop negative feelings as an officer. I've dealt with serious anxieties in the past and some will always have to be under constant control in the background. When I was first fulfilling the officer role, I started unconsciously grinding my teeth while sleeping to the point of seriously damaging them. I later learned from my dentist this is a condition called Bruxism, which can surface from serious anxiety.

Thankfully, I was able to get my fears under control and it did not last! Yes, what we do as officers creates a lot of stress. These stresses can present themselves physically or be housed subconsciously. How can we as officers limit our exposure to these unwanted stresses while we are still under so many other forms of pressure? How can we deal successfully with feelings of inadequacy and job performance anxiety?

One of the most stressful times for an officer is when they first step into the role. There are so many questions that run through your head, so many "what ifs?" I had many of these when I first became a Captain. There were some serious fire hazards in the zones that I would be responding to. Could I really be responsible for protecting life, property, and the environment to such a high standard at all of those locations, and for any emergency? What would failure look like? What if I was responsible for injuring or killing someone accidentally?

These are very healthy fears, but left unchecked, these fears can paralyze you to the point where you as the officer can regress into micromanagement, loss of control, or straight up inaction. How can you gain control of fear? Let me share what has worked for me.

Always Err on the Side of Safety

Your job as an officer is to protect the lives of your crew, the citizens, and yourself over all else. The aid you provide to the public aside, you can say that as the officer, you have had a very successful shift when you are able to send your whole crew (including yourself) home safe and healthy. Your job and the jobs of your firefighters are inherently risky, and you have all agreed to those inherent risks when you put on the uniform. As the officer, you will be placed in difficult positions often, where you must decide to ask your crew to take appropriate risk to be able to accomplish what must be done. There is no way around it. So, beyond the "risk a lot to save a lot principle," what are some more ways you can minimize risk?

Make sure you and your crew are up-to-date and extremely proficient in using the safety equipment that is provided to you. Confirm that all your safety equipment is cared for properly and works to manufacturers' specifications. Do research and make recommendations for better, safer equipment through the proper channels within the department.

Identify and understand the major risks in your run area. Brainstorm with your crew ways to minimize those major risks before the alarm to respond to them rings. Consider creating laminated cards on responding to those target areas that are thought out, concise, and can be referred to and easily understood under stressful circumstances.

Do research on different, or new, safety practices through training videos and periodicals. Reflect on line of duty deaths, after action reports, and calls with favorable outcomes for ways you can improve your methods of scene mitigation. Ask other experienced officers how they balance safety and the duty to act.

You must constantly reevaluate risks within your run zone and within your jurisdiction. More importantly, you must reevaluate risks as they change on scene to continuously ensure that you are never risking a lot for a little. This mind set must be the priority in your strategies and tactics. Can you think of more ways to be properly safe? If you can employ these tactics and more, many unhealthy fears will dissipate.

Fear is Normal

Realize that having a fear of the unknown is human and necessary. No one at the fire department, even the best of officers and firefighters, is superhuman or above fear. Any rational person has a strong sense of self preservation. Having a healthy amount of fear is important. You need that fear on your mind constantly, but it must be under control and in the background. Think of it as a guard dog. You want your guard dog to protect your property, but never attack you! Qualified guard dogs need serious continuous training to be competent and safe. How can you train your fear to protect you?

Figure out what you are afraid of specifically and attack it head on. Is there a certain target hazard in your zone that keeps you up at night? Maybe something as nuanced as an airport? Take ARFF – Aircraft Rescue & Fire Fighting specific classes, do airport building surveys, or ask pilots to train you on on-board aircraft fire control systems. Gain knowledge and train until it's no longer a debilitating fear.

Make a prioritized list of your biggest fears and what brings you the most anxiety in your jurisdiction. For each one, research, train, and practice possible responses to those hazards. The more you know, the more comfortable you will be, and the more you will bring your fears under control.

Create a prioritized list of fears the crew may have. Learn as much as you can about any threat you may encounter together. Knowledge is power! Let it help you gain confidence built on team adeptness. Look back through call logs to see what types of emergencies have already occurred and their outcomes. Try and predict what formidable events are likely to occur in the future, and train and practice on all of these possible events until you become proficient. Share what you have learned through training with your department so others can be empowered. Identifying your fears and preparing your attack as a crew can put any daunting fears in their proper place.

Do What's Right

Always do what is right and have nothing to fear. Officers are constantly tasked with making decisions using minimal, if any, pertinent information coupled with significant time constraints. Often, these decisions can be the difference between a life-or-death outcome. There is only so much your protocols, experiences, and guidelines can do to help you in your decision-making process. Therefore, how can you make the best choices with the fear that those choices could cause harm and/or be closely scrutinized?

After you have weighed the risks versus the rewards and reflected on your prior knowledge and training, do what is *right*. What is "right?" Most likely it is the hardest thing to do, which is the reason people often fail to do it. What is "right" can be very nuanced and is different to everyone according to their specific bias or belief system. To find the closest version of "right" you can in any situation, you must use a heaping dose of empathy.

Empathy is the ability to understand and share the feelings of another. It is the golden rule: Treat others the way you would like to be treated. Obviously, there is room for error here. You cannot possibly know the exact way someone wants to be treated, or the feelings they are feeling, but empathy will bring you closest to the mark. You must implement empathy in your decision-making process when appropriate. It is a powerful ally to not only making the right choice, but also to defending your choices to even the harshest of critics, which is often you.

If you are making a decision regarding patient care, put yourself or a comparable loved one in that patient's position. Are you giving the care you would expect to receive? Most likely you have a very high-standard of what that care entails. Will the care you are about to provide meet those standards or go beyond? If you are directing a firefighter to participate in a dangerous activity, how would you respond to the same direction?

If you were in the position to make a choice effecting the protection of someone's property, how would you expect your property to be cared for? Making decisions this way will protect you from making ones that are indefensible, or just plain wrong. Using empathy in your choices helps you to create better outcomes not just for you, but more importantly, your crew and the public you serve. Yes, empathy is key to reducing fear through better decision making.

Be Truthful

Honesty is a fear killer. You must be truthful in all your endeavors as an officer. Being dishonest, even once, can undo the hard work you've done to generate trust among your crew and your department. How does honesty limit fear? Even a small amount of dishonesty can give birth to many lies. Why allow yourself to have such heavy weights hanging over your head ready to fall at any moment? Nothing is truly gained by being dishonest, but much can be lost. Covering lies brings fear of being discovered.

Dishonesty is very dangerous in a profession where we have been given the public's trust. The citizens of our communities open their homes to us for help in times of their most dire circumstances. You as an officer owe it to them to honor that trust with the most honest crew you can muster.

You also owe honesty to your crew. Throughout your tenure as their officer, you will be putting them in harm's way. Your crew must know that you are honest to be able to trust you. Show them you are honest. Your example in this will help your crew to be honest as well. Let your crew know you want them to be open and honest with you in all things pertaining to their job, then use that knowledge to help and protect them to the best of your abilities.

If you have lied in the past, come clean, apologize, and make it right. Do what it takes to mend the relationships that may be damaged. Although this would understandably be very uncomfortable, carrying the weight of that lie on your shoulders and the fear it imposes on you for a career is more agonizing. Don't give excuses. Excuses are a sign of internal weakness and that you are not truly taking responsibility for your actions. Be strong, have pride, take responsibility, care for your inner self, and your fellow firefighters will see someone they can respect and follow. Let honesty protect you from unnecessary fear.

Trust What You've Built

Fall back on what you've worked so hard to build and on those you trust. It's time to trust in the team you have been building. Trust in the planning you've done, the healthy communication you've had, the training you've provided, and the team you've assembled. When you have a talented crew around you, fear will melt away.

If your team is not quite ready, get them there. It is much like weathering a hurricane in a well-built home. When the foundation to the roof is engineered to withstand the strongest of storms, its occupants can rest easy. The same goes for you and your crew. Continuously fortify your crew's craftsmanship and unity. When the major incidents come, you will be able to trust in the skills of your crew, and fear will be suppressed and put securely in its place.

Fall back on a trusted mentor or experienced officer. I was a hazardous materials technician when I became an officer, so by default, I was then an officer at a hazardous materials (HazMat) station. My department provides a HazMat team as part of a regional response with other jurisdictions that surround our city. As a fledgling officer of the HazMat team, I had many fears. It is unnerving to respond to adjacent municipalities you are not familiar with, much less perform specialty work in front of firefighters you've never met.

To deal with all the uncertainties I had, I reached out to my mentors and the other hazmat officers. I let them know I had reservations and asked them if I could reach out to them on an emergency scene if needed. All of those officers readily agreed to make sure they were available for assistance when I was on duty as the HazMat Officer. There were a few times when I called them for advice on a hazardous materials incident. That accessibility and knowing they were available as a resource even if I didn't need them, helped quench my fears. You can do the same. Reach out to your mentors and subject experts. Set up the ability to use them if the appropriate moment arises.

Never Surrender

Never give up on attaining your goals. Striving towards a goal gives purpose and a specific target to focus on. Having a target in sight dispels fear. Picture a pilot who is attempting a landing in extremely low visibility. The pilot's goal is to find the runway, but it is shrouded in clouds. What do you think will happen to the level of fear that pilot will feel if the cloud cover breaks, and the pilot can see the runway clearly? That fear will no doubt dissipate back to background levels, and it will be business as usual for the landing.

Keep your goals visible. Make a map or list that is visible to the crew. Speak positively of your efforts to reach those goals. Keep the finish line firmly in your mind's eye, focus on the essential strategies to accomplish it, and fear will disappear.

Achieving a goal builds confidence, and confidence is a powerful antidote to fear. The successes that you have along with your crew will help you to repel feelings of inadequacy. Celebrate your accomplishments as a crew, and rely on your sharpened capabilities. Do not let those capabilities dull. Together, create new goals to attain.

That being said, not all goals stand the test of time and changing circumstances. At times you will need to reevaluate your goals and change them to be more specific to the crew's needs. Make known the changes and how they will be better suited to guide the crew, and make sure everyone is abreast of the new plan with opportunities for input. This is quite the opposite of giving up on a goal, it is called leadership!

When duty calls, you are expected to get your crew to the incident fast and make quality decisions to mitigate that event to the safest, most beneficial outcome. You are expected to perform to that high standard of response *every* time. This is no small feat. Stopping feelings of inadequacy and fear is a constant battle, especially when responding to high stress incidents.

Use these concepts to gain the confidence needed to kill the fear and anxiety that breeds poor leadership and inaction. As you become more experienced, add to these concepts and share them with others. Implement what you've learned to put any negative feelings you or your crew may have in their proper places.

Chapter Seven

Attitudes Are What Really Matter

E ach of your crew members will approach their job differently and express themselves according to their own life experience and accumulative internal feelings. Each person is an amalgam of their cultural background, the beliefs they hold, and the hardships or achievements they have had in their life. As they interact with the world in different ways, their life experience creates and molds their perspectives. Perspectives then bond to form a prevalent attitude that they show to the world through behavior. Attitudes reflect the deepest self or the seed of motivation of the individual. How can the attitudes of your subordinates affect your approach to leadership?

What type of firefighter would you rather have on your crew? One with a poor attitude and great skills, or one with a great attitude and poor skills? In my experience, I would much rather have a firefighter with a great attitude and poor skills every time. Why?

First off, what do I mean by "great attitude?" For the purpose of this chapter, a great attitude entails the following qualities: Overall positivity, a healthy work ethic, readiness to learn, determination in achieving goals, openness to change, and pride in work output no matter the import. Give me a firefighter like that, and it would be hard to fail to teach them even the toughest of skills.

Therefore, it is imperative that you are not putting the cart before the horse so to speak. First comes the correct attitude, and then comes the ability to learn skills and use them appropriately in the long-term. Firefighters have many skills and abilities, but they must have a desire to maintain and use them well. Skills cannot stand on their own. They need the right attitude to make them potent. The attitudes of your firefighters are what really matter! Prioritize the attitudes of your firefighters over training their skills.

When you focus on grooming their attitudes, the skills and abilities will follow.

You as an officer will expend a large portion of your time wrangling attitudes. With a firehouse full of unique and complex attitudes, how can you influence each individual to be positive about their work, your department, and you as their officer? You cannot rewrite the histories and experiences of each of your firefighters, nor should you. What then, can you focus on to facilitate the correct attitudes you need in the firehouse?

Get Your Head Right

The correct attitude starts with you. You cannot expect your crew to maintain a positive attitude if your attitude stinks. Your attitude must be an example. You cannot hold your firefighters to a different standard than the one you have for yourself. You must constantly and carefully maintain your attitude first. How can you improve your attitude?

Now is the time to showcase the qualities we have discussed in the first few chapters. You will need these qualities to realign your perspectives in a positive way and display self-control. Be ever aware of how your perspectives are affecting the way you present yourself to others. Consider your own attitude toward daily station life, and the specific areas of attitude adjustment you are trying to achieve with the crew.

Perhaps they are following the example you are currently demonstrating, and you need to revise your attitude. What attitude do you manifest when faced with changes? How do you approach training from the department? How do you handle conflict? What changes can you make for a more exemplary attitude for your firefighters to emulate? Use the advice from chapter 2 to help you to work hard at continually transforming your attitude so it can be the benchmark for all others.

You can help foster a proper attitude by how you handle complaints. Complaints should only be sent up the chain of command and not down. Valid complaints about the way your department does business, and ways it could be improved, should be communicated tactfully to those that are in the position to address them. When you facilitate a complaint in this manner, it becomes a recommendation. Recommendations are positive and help in securing better work conditions.

The same is not true when you voice complaints down the chain of command to your firefighters. Complaining down to your crew about the department creates a negative atmosphere that can dissolve good attitudes quickly. Most likely, the firefighters of your crew are not in the position to change the issue. Complaining to them will poison their view of it and demonstrate that you are not taking useful action to facilitate actual change.

Your job is to help lead your crew with the directives you receive from those that ultimately employ you and your crew. If you convince them those directives are invalid, you have just led them away from the departmental standard. Lead them to overcome adversity or disagreement over departmental policy with proper action, not complaints. Even when those complaints are valid and vocalized respectfully, they will still have the same negative effect on your subordinates. If you complain about your supervisors in front of your crew, sooner or later, they will complain about you. Do your best not to fall into this trap.

Complaining has been a struggle for me from time to time. There are many things that could have been done better, or handled more tactfully, within my own fire department. The natural "knee jerk" reaction is to complain about something that displeases or irritates you. When that happens, I have to force myself to stop and think about the damage it does to the hard work I've put into gaining respect from my peers and the department itself.

We all complain, it's human nature. It means that we care. Let that care motivate us to positive action instead. Never let a complaining attitude corrupt you or your crew. Strengthen your self-control to weed out complaints before they happen.

Finally, shore up your positive attitude with some enthusiasm. Get excited about what you do. What made you want to be a firefighter? Embody that feeling and bring some energy to the station. You could have the best attitude in the world, but if you sit around expressionless with no energy who is going to notice or care?

You don't have to be manic or fake. Just have fun. That kind of energy is contagious and it's a petri dish for great attitude growth. People want to be excited, and when the crew is excited, work is enjoyable and it is easier to get through the mundane tasks and forget about the negative influences that may be pressuring the crew towards a poor attitude.

Your Crew's Attitude

Gain an overall perspective on the way the crew conducts themselves. Is it net positive or net negative? The answer to that question should become blatantly clear with even a minimal amount of observation.

Here are some key areas to look at closely that will better reveal any hidden issues.

Most likely you are already keenly aware of how each member of your crew treats each other, but how do they treat those that are on exchange or float in for the shift? Do they afford them the same respect they give to each other even if that person may not be very talented or outgoing? Do they treat them as a guest and offer assistance navigating the nuances of the crew's way of operating?

These questions are important, not just for a fire-fighter level position, but also for officers that fill your position while you are off duty, or perhaps stepping up into a higher role. Make it a point to contact those that float into your station and get their honest view on how your crew treated them. Make it clear to them that they will remain anonymous whether it is a good or bad report. Meditate on that report to find ways to improve the crew.

How does the crew treat probationary employees? Do they help the probationary employee establish new skills? Do they disrespect the probationary employee when you are not present? Although there are discernible differences in the responsibilities of each crew member, no one should be treated poorly. Period.

When the health of the crew is high, it will be easily distinguished by the appropriate respect given to minimally senior members. Be extra vigilant for negative attitudes in this area, as it will be an infection that can spoil the entire environment you've worked hard to nourish. Be the example on how to properly treat *every* member of your crew *impartially*.

Observe your crew when they are speaking to the public on and off emergency calls. What kind of message are they sending with the words and body language they choose to exhibit? How would you feel if that message was directed to you or your family? Are there areas of improvement that need to be handled? There are infinite small ways we can improve our customer service on any call, many with minimal effort.

Do the members of your crew go above and beyond when possible and without direction? Or do they find ways to escape doing more? Losing the desire to make the lives of the people we serve better is a late sign of an ugly underlying issue of negativity. Often when one firefighter starts to approach work in this way, the others follow suit. Be ever aware of this poor attitude from any crew member and address it before it spoils the bunch.

Each Crew Member

Now that you have carefully curated your own attitude and understood your crew as a whole, you can
now move onto understanding the individual attitudes of each of your crew mates. Very often this is
the most difficult endeavor. Since you are fulfilling
the officer's role, chances are you are not new to your
department, and have some, if not a lot of seniority.
Because of this, you may have known some or all of
the members of your crew for a long time. In contrast,
you may be part of a large organization where it's
difficult to know everyone. Or perhaps, you are stepping up, filling in for a vacancy, or newly promoted to
a station where you have a different crew you may not
know very well. Whatever your situation, be aware
that at times, because you are the officer, your subordinates will veil their feelings from you. Because
of this, start from scratch when deciphering each of
your firefighter's attitudes. What are some ways to do
that?

Make a list of the pros and cons of each of your subordinates' attitudes. The goal here is to understand
what attitudes they have presented in the past and
present, so you can create a plan, if needed, for future
ones. Take an honest look at each person. If you are

close to any of your crew, especially outside of work, try and leave that bias behind as you understand their attitude at work. Don't let the fact that they are a friend cloud your judgment. It might be advisable to find a trusted source that is not as close to that firefighter as you and get their honest thoughts.

Don't Assume

If you inherit firefighters who have a reputation that precedes them, take it with a grain of salt. Not every reputation is true. Make your own judgments based on your own experiences and the standards that you are trying to apply. Consider contacting their previous officer to ask if there is any pertinent history that will help you to better understand and help that firefighter. If possible, review the past performance evaluations of each individual. The point is to gain a decent idea of each person's work history so you can compare it with their current approach to work.

Be observant around the station, and when responding to emergency calls. How does the history that you have collected compare to each individual's current attitude? How does each crew mate treat the others, the patient, their equipment, or the station? Are they ready and willing to work hard on calls? Is their uniform disheveled? How do they carry themselves, and what kind of body language are they presenting? How do they act when they believe no one is watching? How do they react to training or changes? The list could go on forever.

Once you've had at least a few shifts where you were able to observe your individual firefighters in different situations, you can begin to form a general idea of the basic health of each one's attitude. Deeply consider those attitudes, and then generate a decent list of the pros, and hopefully a small number of cons, if any, to address.

Find the Real Motivation

Your next stop is to discover strong motivators for each of your crew members. The fire service has a certain gravity to it that pulls people in. For example, the camaraderie that is to be found, relied upon, and enjoyed. The heritage of working a career your family worked before you or starting off a new family line of firefighters. The traditions and shared experiences steeped in history and handed down through mentorship. The war stories of overcoming odds and saving someone's life. The funny situations that happen just from the mere fact you have such different people living together 24 hours at a time. There are many things that can make a person fall in love with their career as a firefighter and find pride in what they do. Use what they love to motivate them.

Share what makes being a firefighter special to you. Relate why you work in a field where it's very possible your life could be on the line. Tell your crew what is most important in your life and career. Encourage them to share the same about themselves, and truly listen to what they have to say. Without overstepping, have an idea of each of your firefighter's basic backgrounds and family situations. Taking the above into account for each firefighter will help you create an idea of what truly motivates them. Motivation plays a major role in transforming attitudes.

Review all the information you've collected on your crew. Let all the pros you've found really help build on your positive outlook and be thankful for what you have. Thoroughly contemplate the cons. Before approaching anyone about their perceived areas of improvement, again, make sure you are a clear example of those areas you wish to strengthen in them. Make a point of exhibiting the attitude you are looking for around your crew.

Weaponize What Matters

Have a private discussion with each crew member. Commend them for all the great aspects of their work and attitude that adds to the strength of the team. Tactfully address the areas of their attitude that need improvement and be positive about it. Be honest with them about the changes you have made and still need to make, so they feel the discussion is coming from a place of empathy and authenticity. Let them know you are meeting with everyone the same way, and everyone is taking part in building an even better team. Make it understood that you and the crew are an available resource for help. Give them ideas on ways to effect the necessary changes to their attitude.

Reminisce with each of your crew members about what made them fall in love with their career. All of the positives it has brought to their lives and opportunities it has presented. Weaponize those deep attachments by making them a motivator to improve. Describe how those improvements will manifest a perceptible difference for the better, not just for the individual, but for the team, department, citizens, and their own family. Ninety-nine times out of one hundred, approaching a firefighter in this way pays off big time.

This is where all the challenging footwork that you have accomplished comes full circle. You have embodied the qualities of service, sacrifice, self-control, and humility. You put your crew's needs first and made caring for them in a work sense a labor of love. You've been an example of positivity and created an environment that is safe and conducive to growth. You have planned and put into action training, mentorship, and open communication. You have shown trust in your crew by empowering them to work hard using their own abilities and allowing them to take pride in themselves. You have shown you care. You have built a family.

It is not often that anyone, especially a person who dedicates themselves to a career in which they put the lives of others ahead of their own, will ignore a plea to improve from an officer under circumstances like those. Most likely with conditions like the ones outlined above, a firefighter will leap at the opportunity to improve! Yes, it does take a serious amount of blood, sweat, and tears to create, but the power of that creation and the inertia for good it encourages is next to unstoppable. You have created a powerful "buy in" with your team and they will reward you with loyalty and hard work.

Chapter Eight

The Problem Employee

As firefighters, we juggle a lot of responsibilities that can put extreme amounts of pressure on us. It is a special type of pressure that many in our community do not understand. Dealing with crisis constantly, even when it is not your own, is tiring to the soul. It leads many firefighters to then rely on their fellow peers within the department, their spouses, their loved ones, or anything else that brings them peace.

Throughout their careers, the areas of solace fire-fighters use as a safe haven can be put in jeopardy, or shattered all together, by time and unforeseen circumstances. The pressures felt while caring for emergencies while on duty, however, never go away. Often, when firefighters lose their areas of solace they rely upon for peace, they start to show signs of irritability in the work place, and become less capable of handling compromise or discomfort. They become unhappy.

When firefighters are dispirited, it will show in their work and in their interactions with you and the crew. When a firefighter falls into this state, you as an officer must have your finger on the pulse of the crew to realize it is happening. Always be on the look-out for negative changes and behaviors that manifest themselves within your crew, and around the station.

Sometimes the behaviors that manifest under these conditions can be truly shocking or destructive. These are the moments where you can shine as a true leader, where you can call upon the concepts found in this book, your own life, and in departmental experiences to heal those situations. What kind of leader will you be when faced with these challenges?

Control Yourself

When something goes wrong with one of your fire-fighters, they make a mistake, they break the rules, even doing so blatantly, stop the urge to react impulsively, and control yourself. Losing control tells all who are watching that you are not only unprepared, but incapable to handle the problem. You will lose respect, which will be needed in addressing the situation, and you will be putting that person deep into a defensive mode.

Instead, calmly communicate with that person what the expectation was and how the mark was missed. Depending on the gravity of the situation and how time sensitive the matter is, give yourself a moment to cool off. It is time to think and investigate.

Investigate with Empathy

Most likely that person worked very hard to become a firefighter. They took certification courses, they went to fire academy, they may have become an emergency medical technician then a paramedic, etc. That person jumped through the hoops of being hired or accepted as a volunteer. They left their families to then use that body of knowledge and skills to help others for days at a time. Do you really think they woke up the morning of whatever incident you're dealing with and said to themselves "I think I'll blow up my career today?"

What possible influences would make you act in the same manner as that firefighter has? Chances are there is something more at play here. There may be what is called a "core issue" that is causing the poor behavior. Somewhere in that person's life, a chunk of their solace has been broken or destroyed. You as an officer need to find out if there is a core issue at play, understand what that core issue is, and address it. It does not change the fact that the wrong has been committed, however, it will help you to understand how to motivate that person to stop further events. It will also aid in softening their attitude when facilitating the needed changes.

If time allows, and it usually does, prepare your knowledge on the issue at hand. Is there a protocol or rule that was broken? Print it out and re-familiarize yourself with it. Many departments have in-depth policies and procedures. Make sure you are up-to-date on these and know when and how to use them. Consider reaching out to an experienced officer you trust for guidance if you are unsure.

Meet with the troubled crew mate and keep your emotions level. Consider having a benign third party as part of the conversation, such as a union representative, to insure fairness. Relate to them your experience of the issue and what specific behavior was unacceptable. Investigate what motivated them to act in that way. Ask them if they were aware they were behaving poorly, or possibly unaware of the rule or policy they were breaking. Be humble, perhaps there is something you as an officer could have done better to help that firefighter do their job more appropriately.

Get to the heart of the behavior by finding the possible core issue. If that behavior is out of the ordinary for that firefighter, tell them. Ask them what changed to cause them to act in that manner. Use questions that have open ended answers to draw out what could be troubling that crew mate. Phrase those questions in different ways, multiple times, to allow that person ample opportunity to provide the answer. Let them know that if it is something personal, they don't need to give specifics, and it will be kept confidential according to departmental policy. Help them to understand you are not trying to pry into their personal life, but to understand and validate their feelings to help change unacceptable behaviors in the future.

Discipline Means You Care

What would you think of a parent that never disciplines their child? Have you ever been around a child that was never disciplined? It's a nightmare! It's more of a nightmare for that child as they grow up and find they lack the resources to make friends, hold down a job, and be useful in the community. Discipline is meant to guide the recipient back on course when they stray.

The firehouse is not immune to its need. Appropriate discipline is not easy, but it demonstrates you care about that person, the crews they will work with, and the department. By skipping appropriate disciplinary action, you are not doing anyone a favor, and you are undermining your own authority. How can you give discipline fairly and have it affect a real change in the person it is directed to?

Once you have investigated the issue and understand it well, then you can communicate with the errant firefighter how the issue will be rectified. All that may be necessary is a serious conversation. If your department requires disciplinary action, be open and honest with them about the gravity of the situation. Make it perfectly clear if it is a simple issue with minor repercussions, or if it will be a more serious type of progressive disciplinary action. Let them know if the discipline stops with you or must be communicated with your superior officer and above. Outline the specific steps that must be taken as part of your departmental policy and answer any questions the firefighter may have about each one.

Sometimes you may need to call upon other resources of help, especially when a core issue is found that needs delicate care when addressing. Be aware of what resources are open and available to your firefighters through your department, city, state, and government. You may be surprised at what your department or program offers, and how it can aid you in helping your firefighters.

If you have an Employee Assistance Program available to you, find out what it offers and who is eligible. They can offer anything from childcare to dealing with addiction. Does your department have a CISM – (Critical Incident Stress Management team) or the like for dealing with emotionally charged events and Post Traumatic Stress Disorder? Are you familiar with the FMLA (Federal Medical Leave Act)? It can be used for more than just a personal injury, but also welcoming a new baby into the world, or taking time to care for an aging parent. If appropriate, could this be an issue where fellow firefighters from your crew or around the department could handle with a helping hand?

Whatever the case, these avenues of help, along with your departmental disciplinary procedures, should be well in mind before you need to use them. Always re-examine these resources, along with your standing disciplinary procedures, to do what is right for the specific situations that arise. To the best of your ability, customize the plan to be as successful as possible for that individual firefighter. Your main goal is to guide that person past the issue quickly and back to a healthy mindset where work can be done well and with pride.

Do Not Be a Robot

It is no secret that giving and receiving discipline is difficult. Emotions will be high and most likely on display. You must control your emotions to be an example of the behavior you expect. Controlling your emotions does not mean you will not show emotion at all. It means you will show the appropriate emotions for the setting. Again, if you were sitting opposite the officer in this situation, how would you like to be addressed? In what way could it be delivered so that you would be more apt to listen, not become defensive, and make the appropriate changes?

Always use straightforward, clear, tactful, and transparent language when giving counsel. Under extremely delicate circumstances, consider using the "sandwich" method if appropriate. This is a method where you sandwich constructive criticism, or re-alignment of expectations, between encouragement or compliment. It is meant to drop the individual's defensive posture, open them to a new idea or direction, and leave them with a positive feeling. If you use this method, do not be fake. It does not give you the right to give them a "crap" sandwich, where you stick a harsh criticism between phony compliments. Consider your words before you speak by placing yourself in their place. You may reconsider your choice of words.

Give special attention to your body language. Make sure you are taking an open and welcoming posture. A posture where your arms are not crossed, you are turned toward that person, and you are making eye contact with them. Make sure your words are not harsh and it's clear you care about a positive outcome. Show your empathy for that person and the care you have for them by treating them like a human being, not just a cog in the departmental machine. Make them feel needed, and they will feel the need to better themselves and rise to the occasion.

The Agreement

Your goal in these situations is to make sure the fire-fighter understands this is an opportunity for improvement. The firefighter receiving the correction needs to agree that the correction was necessary in order for them to truly want to change it. The negotiation of that agreement falls squarely on you. This is another situation that is very similar to changing a poor attitude.

The healthy station environment you've created and the rapport you've worked hard to establish will be paramount. It creates a strong respect for you and the crew that will hopefully compel that firefighter to be more easily motivated to correct the issue. If not, refer to what really matters to them and have them utilize it as an important reason for change. Take the concept for changing attitudes in chapter 7 and apply it to getting a "buy in" for changing the poor behavior and gaining the agreement.

Sometimes getting the agreement may not be easy. Most likely more communication will be necessary. Be sure to listen well to your firefighter. They need to know you are receiving the information they are sending, and that you are understanding it. Reiterate your firefighter's position to them, so they know they've been understood.

Many times, the mere fact that they can communicate their issue, feel that it is understood and validated, softens their resolve and they agree to change for the better. This may be a very time-consuming part of the process, with more communication than you originally believed would take place. No matter what, be patient. With communication comes understanding, with understanding comes action.

No agreement would be complete without understanding the consequences of breaking that agreement. It would be unfair to the errant firefighter if they did not fully understand the repercussions of persisting with the incorrect behavior. There should be no surprises awaiting that person that they have not been fully prepared for.

You need to understand your department's disciplinary policy so that you can make those repercussions clear to them. This is not meant to be a threatening act. It is done to empower that person with the knowledge of how their actions will affect them in the future, so they can make appropriate decisions regarding their career.

The Plan

Once you attain an agreement from the firefighter to effect the beneficial change, you can hash out the goals for improvement and a timeline to complete them. If you have done your due diligence, you will have a list of goals for that firefighter to accomplish. Before you plan on using any of the goals, have the firefighter contemplate what goals they think would be most beneficial for them. They know themselves better than you do, and you may be surprised by the goals they wish to set for themselves. When the goals are their idea, they will be more disposed to accomplishing them. Once you have an idea of the goals they would like to set, you can then introduce your goals if still relevant.

The goals you pick together should be attainable just like the goals discussed in chapter 4 of this book. Whether you use the SMART method or not, the goals need to be specific to, and useful for, effecting the proper change to create a better version of that firefighter when they are completed. If the goals set are excessively difficult without reason, you will be setting that person up for failure. Deeply consider the abilities of that person and make sure the goals set are customized well for them, feasible, and rational.

Don't over-complicate the timeline for the goals you set. In most instances you will only need one goal and an appropriate amount of time to accomplish it. If the issue is more complicated with multiple steps, you may need more time. Whatever the case, keep the first time frame brief, like a shift or two, and attach it to the most easily met goal. Reaching the first goal quickly will hopefully give that firefighter a taste of its full accomplishment, and drive them to complete the subsequent harder goals. Be aware of their progress and keep them on track. Make sure you and your crew give plenty of positive reinforcement as they progress.

Reevaluate the plan as it unfolds. Never become pigeon-holed into any method, goal, or timeline, and be ready to shift into a more useful modality if that need becomes apparent. Communicate the changes with the firefighter, make sure they are understood, agreed upon, and update the timeline if warranted.

Your job is to help the firefighter succeed. A lousy firefighter evaluation often reflects the poor leadership of the officer. Good leaders rarely write poor evaluations if they are helping their firefighters to be great. Keep that in mind and be there with a helpful hand throughout that person's betterment process. Give that person the tools to succeed and put them in the right position to do so.

Use the resources available to you within your crew as well. If you have another crew member that can be an example to that firefighter in the area of their weakness, have that strong crew member mentor them. In the end, you will be left with two stronger crew members and a closer bond within the team.

Commend, Inspire, Review

When the dust settles and the goals have been achieved, meet with the firefighter, and review the process. Don't be afraid to be heavy handed with the commendations. That person just accomplished a change, not just in their attitude but in their commitment to the crew and the department. They may also have overcome a serious hurdle in their personal life regarding a "core issue" that was affecting them. How would you feel after you have worked hard to change your attitude and improve upon yourself in the face of personal issues? Make it known that the effort they put forth was not lost on you and was fully appreciated.

Challenge the firefighter to continue their path of self-improvement. Give recommendations on ways they can add more value to the team. Find out what areas they would like to improve upon and encourage them to do so. Use the high they may be feeling of reaching their goals to boost them into reaching more.

Review your method. In what areas were your methods strong, and where were they weak? How can you make the process better for the next time a problem arises? Consider relating the process you used to a knowledgeable resource to get an experienced opinion on how it was handled.

Your duty as a leader is to impartially make every member of your crew successful. Don't leave any of it to chance, especially with situations as delicate as discipline. Disciplinary situations can make or break officers and their firefighters. Do not run from giving discipline when it is needed. Be an officer that leads their firefighters out of trouble when it arises and makes them stronger. When each crew member is stronger, the team is stronger. When the team is stronger, there will be much less of a need for discipline.

Chapter Nine

Silent Killers

About a decade into my career, something changed. It was not noticeable to me at first, but I was becoming irritable, closed off, and would sometimes have uncharacteristic swings in my temperament. My wife caught on to the changes in my behavior right away and pointed them out to me. She would often ask me if there was something bothering me or on my mind. I would always reply with the same answer, that there was nothing out of the ordinary in my thoughts, and really, there wasn't.

Little things were starting to make me lose my patience quickly and respond aggressively. It got to the point where I was now noticing my behavior changing, for no perceivable reason, and I knew something was wrong. My wife suggested I had PTSD (Post Traumatic Stress Disorder) but how could that be when I did not feel depressed? How could I have PTSD after only ten years?

The ugly truth is PTS (Post Traumatic Stress) is a part of our lives and jobs as firefighters the very first day we report for duty. Imagine the first duty day a rookie firefighter on 9/11/2001 with the Fire Department of New York City had. Do you think that rookie would have good reason to have PTS after only their first shift? I understand that may be considered an extreme example, but major traumatic events can happen and do happen every day we are on duty. There is no magic time frame for when the effects these events have on us will reveal themselves, but they will. We need to come to terms with the reality that every first responder who dons the uniform and answers the call *will* deal with PTS.

I am going to make a clear disclaimer here and now that I am not a trained clinician on the subject of PTS and PTSD. The concepts that I discuss in this chapter are learned from dealing with my personal encounters with PTS, and the tactics that have worked for me at the station level for helping my crew mates.

In my experience, most if not all departments and officers are woefully under prepared to deal with these crises. The proof is in the unprecedented amount of suicide and addictions that plague our profession.[1] PTS is different for everyone it effects, and often those effected may not realize it is PTS or will hide the fact that they are suffering from it.

Historically, our profession has wrongfully been under the impression that being affected emotionally by the atrocities we see while mitigating emergencies is a sign of mental weakness. Really, the above word "see" does not do it justice. We *feel* those atrocities with all of our senses, and those feelings are imprinted into our memories of those incidents. No sane person can consistently deal intimately with grisly emergencies, feel nothing, and walk away without some kind of harmful baggage.

Let's face it, you are most likely not going to put down this book and apply to become a psychiatrist specializing in PTS and PTSD. So, what can you do as a fire officer to protect yourself and crew as much as possible from it?

Be Honest with Yourself

Most likely, if you are fulfilling the role of officer, you are not new to the fire department and have had your fair share of traumatic emergencies. Although it may be imperceptible now, in some shape or form you are probably suffering from PTS. Here are some of the risk factors that increase the possibility of suffering from PTS and PTSD according to The National Institute of Mental Health:[2]

- Living through dangerous events and traumas

- Getting hurt

- Seeing another person hurt, or seeing a dead body

- Childhood trauma

- Feeling horror, helplessness, or extreme fear

- Having little or no social support after the event

- Dealing with extra stress after the event, such as loss of a loved one, pain and injury, or loss of a job or home

- Having a history of mental illness or substance abuse

During your average shift you most likely will deal with at least one, if not more, of those risk factors. In your career you may work over three thousand shifts. That is a lot of constant exposure to the risk factors of PTS. The National Institute of Mental Health also states to be diagnosed with PTSD, an adult must have all of the following for at least one month:

- At least one re-experiencing symptom:

- Flashbacks—reliving the trauma over and over, including physical symptoms like a racing heart or sweating

- Bad dreams

- Frightening thoughts

- At least one avoidance symptom:

- Staying away from places, events, or objects that are reminders of the traumatic experience

- Avoiding thoughts or feelings related to the traumatic event

- At least two arousal and reactivity symptoms:

- Being easily startled

- Feeling tense or "on edge"

- Having difficulty sleeping

- Having angry outbursts

- At least two cognition and mood symptoms:

- Trouble remembering key features of the traumatic event

- Negative thoughts about oneself or the world

- Distorted feelings like guilt or blame

- Loss of interest in enjoyable activities

I was able to check off many of those symptoms right off the bat. I get flashbacks of emotional calls that I've been on. I try to avoid those thoughts because they sometimes bring me feelings of guilt. And unfortunately, I have had angry outbursts. I know I have not escaped the grim reality of PTS in my profession. Do you really think that you can go through an entire career and escape all forms of PTS?

The point here is not to make you run screaming to the nearest psychologist, but to agree to and be open to the fact that this is a serious issue that must be addressed, and that you are not immune. You as the officer must understand that there is a good chance this disorder will affect you, or someone on your crew, at some point. You must be open about the realities of dealing with severe incidents and honest about how those calls affect you. Doing so will help you to be more cognizant of calls filled with risk factors and allow you to recognize if and when your crew mates exhibit symptoms of PTS.

Be Honest with your Crew

How can you get your crew mates to open up about calls that have had a negative emotional effect on them? Be the example of honest open communication. Make it a habit to speak to each individual crew member privately after every serious incident. Be aware of what PTS risk factors were present during that call and make a note of which ones may have upset that crew member.

Open up to each firefighter about your own feelings regarding the incident, and how you've dealt with those issues in the past. *Show* them that it is okay to be upset when bad things happen. Listen intently to what they say, and gauge how they are dealing with it. Validate their feelings and offer commendation on the work they did during that emergency.

Remember, just because you may not have been affected by that particular call, it does not mean that same call will not be devastating for someone else. Everyone has their own unique set of experiences and circumstances. Even a seemingly routine incident may have triggered a serious reaction from any one of your crew members depending on their past. Help your crew to understand the seriousness of PTS and the damage it can do. Encourage them to speak about incidents that affect them, and never allow anyone in your crew to belittle another because of the way they were affected by a distressful emergency event.

Know the Baseline

My wife was able to recognize that I was suffering from PTS because she cares about me and has a vested interest in me. In order to recognize the signs that one of your crew mates is developing an issue, you have to care about them and have a vested interest in them as well. When you care about someone, you're interested in their ideas, their mood, how they present themselves, etc. When something is out of the norm, you will usually pick up on it right away. When you become aware of these changes, and they become a constant, do not ignore them.

Our usual tendency is to run from confrontation, but addressing a change in a crew member is more important than avoiding the possibility of confrontation. Would you ever want one of your firefighters to resort to some type of destructive behavior when you could have helped? Firefighter safety is not just wearing personal protective equipment and getting annual physicals. It is mental too. You must be familiar with each one of your firefighter's mental baselines and be attentive to harmful changes in them. Great leaders do not fear uncomfortable conversations and do what's necessary to help.

Plan Ahead

There are ways you can limit the amount of risk factors your crew members are exposed to. An obvious one is to train hard on known weaknesses. We have one shot to do the best job we can when the chips are down. Limiting mistakes on calls through proper training has helped my crews come back from some very gruesome incidents feeling like they could not have done it any better.

No one wants to regret a failure, especially one tied to a negative outcome on an emotionally charged call. There is a level of solace in knowing you did your best. Give your crew the tools they need to feel that way after difficult calls. Commend them for being part of a team that works hard to help others in their time of need, even when the outcome is heartbreaking.

Get to know the previous tragic events in your firefighters' lives, and if they are currently dealing with one. Before every shift look at your roster for the day. Decipher if anyone of them has something in their past or present that would make it difficult for them to handle a certain risk factor. If there is, find possible ways to shield that firefighter from them.

For example, I had a crew with a firefighter that had just lost a family member to an overdose. Unfortunately, we respond to overdoses in our run zone frequently. When I saw that firefighter on my roster, I made a plan to speak to that firefighter privately after roll call about their emotional readiness to handle an overdose emergency if it arose. Obviously, that firefighter's emotions were still raw from their loss, and they agreed it would help to find ways to limit them on overdose specific events.

Until that firefighter was ready to return to normal, I did my best to find ways to limit that firefighter's exposure to overdose emergencies. I would have that firefighter scribe on scene instead of being hands on, or have that firefighter stay away from the patient all together when we had enough man power. In the end, we both believed that putting that plan in place helped.

Be ever aware of any risk factor susceptibility your crew members may have. Limit their exposure to those risk factors when it does not detract from the level of service you are providing and it is within your power to do so. If you plan on limiting them on specific calls, let them know your intentions, and make sure they agree with your plan before you implement it.

Don't Wait

Officers are only the first stop in dealing with PTS. Although you as an officer can help through awareness and basic support, you are probably not trained to do much more. As soon as you see symptoms of PTS, be quick to aid your firefighter or crew in finding an entity with the right credentials to help. Be familiar with what resources are possibly available to you and your crew. Does your department have a Critical Incident Team or an Employee Assistance Program? If not, are there resources outside your department in the form of a public or government program? If the resources available to you are lacking, be proactive in improving them.

Sometimes, there is no need to wait or ask if the emergency event had a negative effect, it is blatantly self-evident. If the emergency call your crew just returned from was extraordinarily distressful, such as, the loss of a child, a mass causality event, or an active shooter event, get trained help immediately. If possible, put your unit(s) out of service and await the arrival of that assistance so your crew has time to collect themselves. Recovering from major events like those require adequate specialty care and recovery time without delay.

The Other Suspects

PTS and PTSD is not the only evil that may attach itself to one of your crew members. You also need to be on the lookout for drug addiction and alcoholism. You may be surprised to know that in Americans over the age of twelve, alcohol abuse effects over 20% of people and drug abuse effects over 5% of people.[3]

Substance abuse can destroy a firefighter's career, life, and family very quickly. It is at least, if not more, dangerous than PTS and PTSD. Unfortunately, some firefighters use these destructive habits in an attempt to numb the effects of PTS and PTSD. Even though you may know your firefighters outside of the fire department, it may be hard to detect substance abuse because it is usual for the abuser to hide the addiction. Some of the signs to recognize substance abuse are as follows:

- Increased aggression or irritability

- Changes in attitude/personality

- Lethargy

- Depression

- Dramatic changes in habits and/or priorities

The modality of help you would use for aiding a firefighter with PTS and PTSD is very similar to that of substance abuse. Know the resources available to you, keep an awareness for the signs and symptoms of substance abuse, investigate whether there is truly a problem, tactfully confront that firefighter about the issue, and guide them to find the appropriate help. If you do find that one of your crew mates has a substance abuse addiction, be empathetic. Again, there may be a core issue that is plaguing that firefighter.

If you were to find one of your firefighters under the influence of a non-disclosed non-prescription drug or alcohol while on duty, remove them from duty immediately, give them the chance to seek help, and follow your departmental or city policy on dealing with substance abuse in the workplace. Put an emphasis on getting that person's life back on track by being an advocate for them and facilitating access to appropriate therapy. Treat them as if they were one of your family members.

These concepts are just the tip of the ice burg. There is so much more for any officer to learn regarding these issues that can unfortunately plague us. These will be some of the most delicate areas you will ever deal with. Whatever happens, be empathetic and treat others how you would want to be treated. Make sure you are well prepared for these events if and when they come. If you can lead yourself, as well as your crew, through the perils of these fearsome realities, you will truly be an incredible officer.

Chapter Ten

Keep Your Motor Runnin'

H ave you ever assembled, or seen on television, a performance motor built from the engine block up? It becomes immediately clear that there is a necessary body of knowledge required before you can even attempt the build. Then, you have to collect the right parts and use careful skill when installing them in their specific order. Once the performance motor is assembled, you have to make sure all the parts work in conjunction together smoothly and confirm no mistakes were made during the assembly process.

At times, you may have had to contact another mechanic for advice if you ran into a snag. In the end, when you turn the key and that engine rips on and purrs, wow, what a feeling! The moment when your crew really comes together like a well-oiled machine is like that. It is one of the most satisfying moments you can have in your career as an officer. Seeing hard work pay-off is never disappointing.

But in reality, your work has just begun. All the concepts and advice discussed in this short book will hopefully be just enough to get the engine running, the rest is up to you. The information found in these pages is just a jump start to much more learning ahead. There is no body of work that can encompass everything you would need to know as a leader in the fire department.

So, learn from every resource you can get your hands on. Not everything you read will translate well to your unique set of circumstances, and you might not even agree with some of what this book or other resources claim. Whatever the case, glean what will help you to develop into the best officer you can be.

Every engine, no matter how perfectly engineered and calibrated, will still need tuning and maintenance. Sometimes they may even need to be rebuilt again from the ground up. Always look for ways to keep your engine running in tip top shape. Even when your crew is firing on all cylinders, how can you keep it going strong?

Create a Maintenance Program

Every vehicle has a maintenance schedule issued by the manufacturer. Often, it's called the 30-60-90, because manufacturers usually recommend important check-ups at 30,000, 60,000, and 90,000 miles. When the vehicle owner ignores these and becomes complacent, they usually find themselves walking down the side of the highway with their thumb out because their car broke down. Never become complacent.

Don't ignore the maintenance of your crew. Even when things are running smoothly, put goals on the horizon to achieve. There is always a way to make a great team better. Make your own 30-60-90, set goals for 30, 60, and 90 days out, or perhaps, 30, 60, and 90 months out. Remember, those goals don't have to be overly intense when things are good. Make sure you use balance!

Never Brag

When your crew respects you and each other it creates a cohesive bond and work product that is noticeable. Other officers and firefighters within the department will recognize the quality of your crew's work, and so will the people you serve in the community. Continue to let your crew's product speak for itself. Bragging is ugly, and no one wants to hear it.

Instead, make it clear how hard your firefighters work to make that product a reality. Let people know that you could not have done it without each and every one of your crew members, because you definitely could not have. The crew's output is a testament to your leadership, that is true. Rejoice internally when that output is great, and work on yourself and your leadership methods when it is not up to snuff.

Take Responsibility

Take full responsibility for the failures of your crew. When things don't go well, point the finger directly at yourself. You are the leader, and therefore, have led your crew to that outcome. Do not find clever excuses for the lack of quality that took place. Take credit for the mistakes that happen, even if they were out of your physical control, and stand by your crew.

Obviously, this does have its limits, and you should never put your career in jeopardy for someone who is purposefully negligent. However, if you and your crew did what was right to the best of your abilities with the limited information afforded to you, stand by that product by taking responsibility for it. Showing your crew you will step in front of a proverbial bullet for them will strengthen their respect for you, and teach them to do the same for others. You are responsible for leading your crew to success, but the success belongs to the crew.

Commend

When successes come, find ways to give that recognition to your crew. Write commendations for each of them for the great work they do in the field and at the station. What awards are available to them within your department? What awards are available to them outside the department? Do some research. Help your firefighters to qualify for those awards, and then put in a recommendation for them. Never let an opportunity to recognize the accomplishments of your firefighters go to waste.

Chapter Eleven

Final Thoughts

I hope that you have found some useful insights in your journey as a leader. I hope you can share those insights with others in your crew and within your department. Climbing the mountain of leadership is no easy task. You'll be hard pressed though, to find anything more fulfilling in your career as a firefighter, then leading a healthy crew to help those in need. Be empathetic, always do what's right to the best of your ability, and be safe! Be thankful every day you are empowered to help your community with a group of your friends. There is no better job in the world!

If you enjoyed reading this, please consider leaving an honest review on Amazon. I read every review and they help new readers discover my book.

Endnotes

Chapter 1

(1) Marie S. Mitchell, University of Georgia & Maureen L. Ambrose, "Employees' Behavioral Reactions to Supervisor Aggression: An Examination of Individual and Situational Factors," y, University of Central Florida, July 2012

(2) Susan Krauss Whitbourne Ph.D., "We All Need Role Models to Motivate and Inspire Us," Psychology Today, November, 19 2013, https://www.psychologytoday.com/us/blog/fulfillment-any-age/201311/we-all-need-role-models-motivate-and-inspire-us

Chapter 2

(1) Karen Kangas Dwyer & Marlina M. Davidson, "Is Public Speaking Really More Feared Than Death?," Communication Research Reports Vol. 29, No. 2, April–June 2012, pp. 99–107

(2) Indu Singh, "What Percentage of Communication is Nonverbal?," February 25, 2022,

https://www.helptostudy.com/what-percentage-of
-communication-is-nonverbal/#The_Formula_5538
7

Chapter 3

(1) Various Authors, "Clear Expectations for Kids,"
Focus on the Family, 2022, https://www.focusonthe
family.com/parenting/clear-expectations-for-kids/

(2) The Wellbeing Thesis with Various authors &
references, "The Importance of Taking Breaks,"
https://thewellbeingthesis.org.uk/foundations-for-s
uccess/importance-of-taking-breaks-and-having-ot
her-interests/#:~:text=However%2C%20research%2
0has%20found%20that%20taking%20a%20break,t
aking%20regular%20breaks%20you%20can%20bo
ost%20your%20performance.

(3) 1st Sgt. Brian Baumgartner, "Applicable Team
Building in the Army: Past and Present," Published in
From One Leader to Another Volume II by the U.S.
Army Command and General Staff College in 2015,
May   20,   2020,
https://www.armyupress.army.mil/Journals/NCO-J
ournal/Archives/2020/May/Applicable-Team-Buildin
g/

Army Techniques Publication No. 6-22.6, "Army
Team Building," Headquarters Department of the
Army   Washington,   DC,   30   October   2015,
https://www.armyupress.army.mil/Journals/NCO-J

ournal/Archives/2020/May/Applicable-Team-Buildin g/

(4) Adriana Gattermayr, "Why Healthy Competition Is Key To Cultivating Happiness At Work," Forbes Couches Council, June 14, 2021, https://www.forbes.com/sites/forbescoachescounci l/2021/06/14/why-healthy-competition-is-key-to-cul tivating-happiness-at-work/?sh=5b255b7b56e2

(5) Signe Whitson, "Is Your Child a Limit Tester? Three Essential Steps for Closing Your Loopholes," HuffPost Life, April 25, 2012, https://www.huffpost. com/entry/is-your-child-a-limit-tes_b_1298761

Chapter 4

(1) Professional Leadership Institute, "A Simple 6 Step Process For Setting Smart Goals (With Examples!)," https://professionalleadershipinstitute.com /resources/smart-goal/

Chapter 9

(1) Nina Julia, "Post-traumatic Stress Disorder (PTSD) Statistics: 2022 Update," CFAH, October 5, 2022, https://cfah.org/ptsd-statistics/#PTSD_in_Fir st_Responders

Hope M. Tiesman, PhD; Katherine L. Elkins, MPH; Melissa Brown, DrPH; Suzanne Marsh, MPA; and Leslie M. Carson, MPH, MSW, "Suicides Among First Responders: A Call to Action," Centers for Disease Control & Prevention, NIOSH Science Blog, April 6,

2021, https://blogs.cdc.gov/niosh-science-blog/202
1/04/06/suicides-first-responders/#_edn4

Sara G. Gilman, PsyD, LMFT, "Substance Use
Disorders in First Responders The Vicious Cycle of
Chronic Traumatic Stress Exposure and Sleep
Deprivation as Contributing Factors," NAADAC.org,
Winter   2020,
https://www.naadac.org/assets/2416/aa&r_winter2
020_substance_use_disorders_in_first_responders.
pdf

(2) "Post-Traumatic Stress Disorder," National Institute of Mental Health, May
2022, https://www.nimh.nih.gov/health/topics/pos
t-traumatic-stress-disorder-ptsd

(3) "Drug Abuse Statistics," National Center for
Drug Abuse Statistics, 2022, https://drugabusestatis
tics.org/

Made in the USA
Middletown, DE
31 August 2024

60104192R00087